Edgar Cayce's
Hidden History of Jesus

Edgar Cayce's Hidden History of Jesus

formerly titled
The Greatest Story Never Told

Kirk Nelson

ASSOCIATION FOR
RESEARCH AND
ENLIGHTENMENT

A.R.E. Press • Virginia Beach • Virginia

Formerly published as *The Greatest Story Never Told*

Copyright © 1995 by Kirk Nelson

3rd Printing, April 2000

Printed in the U.S.A.

A.R.E. Press
215 67th Street
Virginia Beach, VA 23451-2061

Library of Congress Cataloging-in-Publication Data
Nelson, Kirk
    [Greatest story never told]
    Edgar Cayce's hidden history of Jesus / by Kirk Nelson.
        p.   cm.
    Originally published : The greatest story never told. Virginia Beach, VA : Wright Pub., 1995.
    ISBN 0-87604-461-5 (trade paper)
    1. Jesus Christ Biography—Miscellanea. 2. Cayce, Edgar, 1877-1945. Edgar Cayce readings. I. Title. II. Title: Hidden history of Jesus.
BT304.93.N45   1999
232.9'01—dc21
[B]   99-40896

Cover design by Lightbourne

Table of Contents

Part One

The Essenes and
Beginning of Jesus' Ministry

I have often thought that if you wanted to make a story confusing, you would write it in ancient English, put portions of it in four different books, and put numbers before every sentence that you write. This, of course, is how we receive the story of Jesus in the Bible.

So I thought, Wouldn't it be nice to have all the events in the life of Jesus contained in one book, arranged chronologically from beginning to end? That is the idea behind this book.

The Bible does not, however, contain all the events in the life of Jesus—there is much we do not know. What were the events that led up to the marriage of Joseph and Mary? How was Jesus educated as a child? Who taught Him? Where did this teaching take place? These are just a few of the events that are not discussed in the Bible.

So, to obtain a complete picture of Jesus' life, we must go to sources of information outside the Bible—specifically, the readings of the Virginia Beach psychic, Edgar Cayce.

The Cayce readings provide us with much of the information about Jesus that is missing from the Bible. They fill in the missing years and give us a great deal of background information about the group of people around Jesus.

In order to give the most complete picture possible of Jesus' life, the four Gospels—Matthew, Mark, Luke, and John—are combined in this book, and the events contained in them are presented largely in chronological order. When the four Gospels describe the same event, only one of the four accounts is used in order to prevent repetition. [Biblical selections have been slightly altered from their translations.] Thus, by combining the four Gospels and filling in the missing years and events with information from the Cayce readings, a near total picture of the life of Jesus can be drawn.

The Essenes

The Cayce readings tell us that Jesus was a member of a strict, pious religious sect known as the Essenes and that this group prepared the way for His birth. Cayce predicted that the writings of this sect would one day be discovered near the Dead Sea. In 1947, two-thousand-year-old scrolls were discovered by Bedouin shepherds in caves on the northwest shore of the Dead Sea. We know them today as the Dead Sea Scrolls. They are the writings of the Essenes, and Cayce accurately predicted where they would be discovered.

The Dead Sea Scrolls describe the organization and beliefs of the Essenes, who had a strict code of moral conduct, including ritual baptism. For this reason scholars have become convinced that John the Baptist was an Essene and that his baptism of Jesus was an Essene ritual. The scrolls also show that the Essenes expected a Messiah who would come to lead the world to righteousness and destroy the wicked. We know this Messiah as Jesus.

The first-century historian, Josephus, describes the Essenes in the following passage:

> There are three sects among the Jews. The followers of the first are the Pharisees; the second the Sadducees; and the third sect, who pretend to a severer discipline, are called Essenes. These last are Jews by birth and seem to have a greater affection for one another than do the other sects. These Essenes reject pleasures as evil, but esteem continence and the conquest of passion as virtue. They neglect wedlock,

but choose out other persons' children while they are pliable and fit for learning; these they esteem to be their kindred and train them according to their own customs. They do not absolutely deny the fitness of marriage and the succession of mankind it provides; but they guard against the lascivious behavior of women and are persuaded that no one of them preserves her fidelity to one man.

These men are despisers of riches, nor is there any one among them who has more than another; for it is law among them that those who join them must let what they have be common to the whole order—to the degree that among all of them there is no appearance of poverty or excess of riches, but every one's possessions are intermingled with every other's; and so there is, as it were, one patrimony among all the brothers. They consider oil a defilement; and if any one of them be anointed without his approval, it is wiped off his body; for they think keeping a dry skin a good thing, and so too being clothed in white garments. They also have appointed to take care of their common affairs stewards who have no separate business except what is for the use of all.

They have no specific city, but many dwell in every city; and if any of their sect come from other places what they have lies open for them just as if it were their own; and they go to such as they never knew before, as if they had been ever so long acquainted with them. For this reason, when they travel into remote parts, they carry nothing with them except their weapons, for fear of thieves. Accordingly, there is, in every city where they live, one appointed particularly to take care of strangers and to provide them with garments and other necessities. But the habit and management of their bodies are such as children use who are in fear of their masters. Nor do they allow the change of garments or shoes till they are entirely torn to pieces or worn out. Nor do they either buy or sell anything to one another; but every one of them gives what he has to him that needs it and receives from him in its stead whatever may be useful for himself; and even if no requital is made, they are fully allowed to take what they need from whomsoever they please.

And as for their piety towards God, it is very extraordinary; for before sunrise they speak not a word about profane matters but offer up certain prayers in supplication received from their forefathers. After this they can be sent away by their curators, to exercise some of those arts wherein they are skilled and in which they labor with great diligence till the fifth hour. After this they assemble in one place; and when they have clothed themselves in white veils, they then bathe their bodies in cold water. And after this purification, they meet together in an apartment of their own, into which no one of another sect is permitted to enter; then they go, in a pure manner, into the dining room, as into certain holy temple, and quietly sit down; the baker lays loaves in order for them; the cook also brings a single plate of one sort of food, and sets it before every one of them; but a priest says grace before meat; and it is unlawful for any one to taste the food before the grace is said. The same priest, after he has dined, says grace again after meat; and when they begin and when they end, they praise God, as He who bestows food upon them; after this they lay aside their white garments and betake themselves to their labors again till evening; then they return home to supper, in the same manner; and if there are any strangers there, they sit down with them. Nor is there ever any clamor or disturbance to pollute their house, but they give every one leave to speak in turn; this silence thus kept in their house appears to foreigners like some tremendous mystery, the cause of which is their perpetual sobriety and the same settled measure as is sufficient of meat and drink allotted them.

And truly, they do nothing not in accordance with the injunctions of their curators; only two things are done among them at every one's free will; to assist those in need and to show mercy; for they are permitted of their own accord to offer succor to such as deserve and need it, and to bestow food on those in distress; but they cannot give anything to their kindred without the curators. They control their anger in a just manner and restrain their passion. They are eminent for fidelity and are ministers of peace; whatsoever they say also is firmer than an oath; but swearing is avoided as being worse than perjury; for they say that he who cannot be believed without swearing by God is already condemned. They also take great pains to study the writings of the ancients and choose out of them what is most for the advantage of their soul and body; and they inquire after such roots and medicinal stones as may cure their diseases . . .

They are long-lived also; many of them living over a hundred years because of the simplicity of their diet and also, I think, because of their regular course of life. They make light of danger and, through the generosity of their mind, are above pain. And as for death, if it be for their glory, they esteem it better than living forever; and indeed our war with the Romans gave abundant evidence of the greatness of their souls under trial even though they were tortured and disfigured, burnt and torn to pieces, and experienced all kinds of instruments of torment so that they might be forced either to blaspheme their legislator or to eat what was forbidden them, yet they could not be made to do either of them, no, nor once to flatter their tormentors or shed a tear; but they smiled in their very pains and laughed those to scorn who inflicted their torments and resigned up their souls with great alacrity, as though expecting to receive them again.

For their doctrine is this: That bodies are corruptible and that their matter is not permanent; but souls are immortal and continue forever, and that they come out of the most subtle ether and are united to their bodies as in prisons, into which they are drawn by a certain natural enticement; but once they are set free from the bonds of the flesh, they then, as if released from a long bondage, rejoice and mount upward. And like the Greeks, they believe that good souls have their habitations beyond the ocean, in a region that is neither oppressed by storms of rain or snow, or by intense heat, but is refreshed by the gentle breathing of a west wind perpetually blowing from the ocean; while they allot to bad souls a dark and tempestuous den, full of never-ceasing punishments. And indeed the Greeks seem to me to have followed the same notion when they allot the islands of the blessed to their brave men, whom they call heroes and demigods; and to the souls of the wicked, the region of the ungodly, in Hades, where, their fables relate, the wicked are punished. This, then, was their first supposition, that souls are immortal; and from thence those exhortations to virtue and warnings against wickedness are collected, whereby good men are bettered in the conduct of their life by their hope of reward after death and whereby the vehement inclinations of bad men to vice are restrained by their fear and expectation that even though they lie concealed in this life they will suffer immortal punishment after death. These are the divine doctrines of the Essenes about the soul, which lay an unavoidable bait for those who have once had a taste of their philosophy.

There are also among them those who undertake to foretell things to come by reading the holy books and using several sorts of purifications, and being perpetually conversant in the discourses of the prophets. And it is but seldom that they miss in their predictions.

Flavius Josephus, Selections from his *Works*
(Abraham Wasserstein, Viking Press)

Edgar Cayce tells us more about the Essenes in the following readings:

> *Ye* say that there were those periods when for four hundred years little or nothing had happened in the experience of man as a revelation from the Father, or God, or from the sources of light. *What* was it, then, that made the setting for the place and for the entering in of that consciousness into the earth that *ye* know as the Son of Man, the Jesus of Nazareth, the Christ on the Cross? Did the darkness bring light? Did the wandering away from the thought of such bring the Christ into the earth? Is this idea not rather refuting the common law that is present in spirit, mind and body that "Like begets like"? As was asked oft, "Can any good thing come out of Nazareth?" Isn't it rather that there were those, that ye hear little or nothing of in thine studies [the Essenes] that dedicated their lives, their minds, their bodies, to a purpose, to a *seeking* for that which had been to them a promise of old? Were there not individuals, men and women, who dedicated their bodies that they might be channels through which such an influence, such a *body* might come?   262-61

> Q. *What is the correct meaning of the term* "*Essene*"?
> A. Expectancy.
> Q. *Was the main purpose of the Essenes to raise up people who would be fit channels for the birth of*

the Messiah who later would be sent out into the world to represent their Brotherhood?

A. The individual preparation was the first purpose. The being sent out into the world was secondary. Only a very few held to the idea of the realization in organization, other than that which would come with the Messiah's pronouncements.

Q. *Were the Essenes called at various times and places Nazarites, School of the Prophets, Hasidees, Therapeutae, Nazarenes, and were they a branch of the Great White Brotherhood, starting in Egypt and taking as members Gentiles and Jews alike?*

A. In general, yes. Specifically, not altogether. They were known at times as some of these; or the Nazarites were a branch or a *thought* of same, see? Just as in the present one would say that any denomination by name is a branch of the Christian-Protestant faith, see? So were those of the various groups, though their purpose was of the first foundations of the prophets as established, or as understood from the school of prophets, by Elijah; and propagated and studied through the things begun by Samuel. The movement was *not* an Egyptian one, though *adopted* by those in another period—or an earlier period—and made a part of the whole movement.

They took Jews and Gentiles alike as members—yes.   254-109

The term *Essene* meant "expectancy"; namely, the expectant birth of the Christ child.

In those days when there had been more and more of the leaders of the peoples in Carmel— the original place where the school of prophets was established during Elijah's time, Samuel— these were called then Essenes; and those that were students of what ye would call astrology, numerology, phrenology, and those phases of that study of the return of individuals—or reincarnation.

These [studies] were then the reasons that there had been a proclaiming that certain periods were a cycle; and these had been the studies then of Arestole, Enos, Mathias, Judas [not Iscariot], and those that were in the care or supervision of the school—as you would term.

These [ideas] having been persecuted by those of the leaders . . . the Sadducees, [who taught] "There is no resurrection," or there is no incarnation, which is what it [resurrection] meant in those periods.

[Then] with those changes that had been as the promptings from the positions of the stars . . . that is the common vision of the solar system of the sun, and those from without the spheres— or as the common name, the North Star . . . this began the preparation—for the three hundred years, as has been given, in this period . . .

In these signs then was the new cycle . . . the beginning of the Piscean age, or that position of the Polar Star or North Star as related to the southern clouds. These made for the . . . symbols; as would be the sign as used, the manner of the sign's approach and the like.

These then were the beginnings, and these were those that were made a part of the studies during that period.

Then there were again . . . the approach of that which had been handed down and had been the experiences from the sages of old—that an angel was to speak. As this occurred when there was the choosing of the mate [Mary] that had—as in only the thought of those so close—been im-

maculately conceived, these brought to the focal point the preparation of the mother.

Then when there were those periods when . . . the priest . . . Zacharias, was slain for his repeating of same in the hearing of those of his own school, these made for those fears that made the necessary preparations for the wedding, the preparations for the birth . . . for those activities for the preservation (physically) of the child; or the flight into Egypt.   **5749-8**

The Essenes were involved with the school of the prophets, which was established at Mt. Carmel by Elijah. The studies there included astrology, numerology, phrenology, and reincarnation—beliefs which were persecuted by the Sadducees who did not believe in the immortality of the soul.

Because of their study of astrology the Essenes realized that the earth was about to change from the Age of Aries to the Age of Pisces and that this change would begin with the birth of the Christ child. Every 2,165 years the earth moves 30 degrees with respect to the background stars, and it is this action which moves the earth from one astrological age to the next. This is called the precession of the equinoxes.

The Essenes were aware that the religious symbols would alter with the change in the ages. During the previous age, the Age of Aries, the religious symbols revolved around the sign of Aries, a fire sign which is symbolized by the ram. The religious rituals which were used then involved sacrificing rams on an altar of fire. This took place in the Jewish temple in Jerusalem and is discussed at length in the Old Testament.

However, this new age, the Age of Pisces, required new symbols and rituals.

Pisces is a water sign symbolized by the fish. When Jesus came, He was the embodiment of the Piscean Age. He was baptized in water, calmed the water, walked on water, changed water into wine, multiplied the fish and the loaves, and was called the "fisher of men." Today, people even use the Greek word for fish, *ichthys*, as a symbol for Jesus. In addition, He suffered martyrdom, and Pisces is the martyr's sign.

Because the Essenes were aware of the changes in the astrological ages and the expectant birth of the Christ child, they prepared twelve girls as possible channels for the birth. Mary was one of the twelve.

Q. Please describe the associate membership of the women in the Essene brotherhood, telling what privileges and restrictions they had, how they joined the Order, and what their life and work was.

A. This was the beginning of the period where women were considered as equals with the men in their activities, in their abilities to formulate, to live, to be, channels.

They joined by dedication—usually by their parents.

It was a free will thing all the way through, but they were restricted only in the matter of certain foods and certain associations in various periods—which referred to the sex, as well as to the food or drink.

Q. How did Mary and Joseph first come in contact with the Essenes and what was their preparation for the coming of Jesus?

A. As indicated, by being dedicated by their parents.

Q. Please describe the process of selection and training of those set aside as holy women such as Mary, Editha, and others as a possible mother for

*the Christ. How were they chosen . . . and what was
their life and work while they waited in the Temple?*
A. They were first dedicated and then there
was the choice of the individual through the
growths, as to whether they would be merely
channels for general services. For, these were
chosen for special services at various times; as
were the twelve chosen at the time, which may
be used as an illustration. Remember, these came
down from the periods when the school had begun, you see.

When there were the activities in which there
were to be the cleansings through which bodies
were to become channels for the new race, or
the new preparation, these then were restricted—
of course—as to certain associations, develop-
ments in associations, activities and the like. We
are speaking here of the twelve women, you
see—and all of the women from the very beginning who were dedicated as channels for the new
race, see?

Hence the group we refer to here as the
Essenes, which was the outgrowth of the periods
of preparations from the teachings by Melchizedek,
as propagated by Elijah and Ilisha [Elisha] and
Samuel. These were set aside for preserving
themselves in direct line or choice for the offer-
ing of themselves as channels through which
there might come the new or the divine origin,
see?

Their life and work during such periods of
preparation were given to alms, good deeds, mis-
sionary activities—as would be termed today.

                                        254-109

Q. How were the maidens selected and by whom?
A. By all of those who chose to give those that

were perfect in body and in mind for the service
. . . each as a representative of the twelve in the
various phases that had been or that had made
up Israel—or man.

*Q. Describe the training and preparation of the
group of maidens.*

A. Trained as to physical exercise first, trained
as to mental exercises as related to chastity, pu-
rity, love, patience, endurance. All of these by
what would be termed by many in the present as
persecutions, but as tests for physical and mental
strength; and this under the supervision of those
that cared for the nourishments by the protection in the food values. These were the manners
and the way they were trained, directed, protected.

Q. Were they put on a special diet?

A. No wine, no fermented drink ever given.
Special foods, yes. These were kept balanced according to that which had been first set by Aran
and Ra Ta.   5749-8

*Q. Does the immaculate conception, as explained,
concern the coming of Mary to Anne, or Jesus to
Mary?*

A. Of Jesus to Mary.

Q. Was Mary immaculately conceived?

A. Mary was immaculately conceived.

*Q. How long was the preparation in progress be-
fore Mary was chosen?*

A. Three years.

Q. In what manner was she chosen?

A. As they walked up the steps!   5749-7

Q. How old was Mary at the time she was chosen?

A. Four; and, as ye would call, between twelve
and thirteen when designated as the one chosen

by the angel on the stair.   5749-8

Mary was chosen as the channel for the birth of Jesus as she climbed the temple steps during the Essenes' morning prayer ritual.

Q. Give a detailed description for literary purposes, of the choosing of Mary on the temple steps.
A. The temple steps—or those that led to the altar, these were called the temple steps. These were those upon which the sun shone as it arose of a morning when there were the first periods of the chosen maidens going to the altar for prayer; as well as for the burning of the incense.

On this day, as they mounted the steps all were bathed in the morning sun; which not only made a beautiful picture but clothed all as in purple and gold.

As Mary reached the top step, then, then there were the thunder and lightning, and the angel led the way, taking the child by the hand before the altar. This was the manner of choice, this was the showing of the way; for she led the others on *this* particular day.

Q. [Was this the angel Gabriel?] Was there any appearance of the angel Gabriel in the home?
A. In the temple when she was chosen, in the home of Elizabeth when she was made aware of the presence by being again in the presence of the messenger or forerunner [John].

Again to Joseph at the time of their union. Again (by Michael) at the time when the edict was given. [flight to Egypt]   5749-7

Q. Was this the orthodox Jewish temple or the Essene temple?
A. The Essenes, to be sure.

Because of the adherence to those visions as proclaimed by Zacharias in the orthodox temple, he (Zacharias) was slain even with his hands upon the horns of the altar.

Hence these as were being here protected were in Carmel, while Zacharias was in the temple of Jerusalem.

Q. Was Mary required to wait ten years before knowing Joseph?

A. Only, you see, until Jesus went to be taught by others did the normal or natural associations come; not required—it was a choice of them both because of their *own* feelings.

But when He was from without the roof and under the protection of those who were the guides . . . these associations began then as normal experiences.

Q. Where the parents of John the messenger members of the band which prepared for Jesus?

A. As has just been indicated, Zacharias at first was a member of what you would term the orthodox priesthood. Mary and Elizabeth were members of the Essenes, you see; and for this very reason Zacharias kept Elizabeth in the mountains and in the hills. Yet when there was the announcing of the birth and Zacharias proclaimed his belief, the murder, the death took place.

Q. Where was the wedding . . . of Mary and Joseph?

A. In the temple there at Carmel.

Q. Where did the couple live during the pregnancy?

A. Mary spent the most of the time in the hills of Judea, portion of the time with Joseph in Nazareth. From there they went to Bethlehem to be taxed, or to register—as ye would term.

5749-8

The birth of John the Baptist is foretold

The story of Zacharias, Elizabeth, and Mary is told to us in the following verses of the Bible:

> In the days of Herod, the king of Judea, there was a certain priest named Zacharias and his wife was named Elizabeth.
>
> They were both righteous before God, walking in all the commandments and ordinances of the Lord.
>
> They had no children, because Elizabeth was barren, and they were both very old.
>
> And it came to pass that it was Zacharias's turn to burn the incense in the temple.
>
> And the whole multitude of people were praying outside at the time of the incense.
>
> Then there appeared to Zacharias an angel of the Lord, standing on the right side of the altar of incense.
>
> And when Zacharias saw him, he was troubled and afraid.
>
> But the angel said to him, Fear not, Zacharias, for your prayer is heard, and your wife, Elizabeth, shall have a son; and you shall call his name John.
>
> And you shall have joy and gladness, and many shall rejoice at his birth.
>
> For he shall be great in the sight of the Lord, and he shall not drink wine or strong drink; and he shall be filled with the Holy Spirit even from his mother's womb.
>
> And many of the children of Israel shall he turn to the Lord, their God.
>
> And he shall go before him in the spirit and power of Elijah, to turn the hearts of the fathers to the children, and the disobedient to the wisdom of the just to make the people prepared for the Lord.
>
> And Zacharias said to the angel, How can this be? For I am an old man, and my wife is old, too.

And the angel said to him, I am Gabriel who stands in the presence of God, and I was sent to tell you these glad tidings.

And, behold, you shall be dumb and shall not be able to speak until the day that these things occur, because you did not believe me.

And the people waited for Zacharias and marveled that he stayed so long in the temple.

And when he came out, he could not speak, and they realized that he had seen a vision because he made signs to them and did not speak.

And after his days of service in the temple, he went home.

And his wife, Elizabeth, conceived and hid herself for five months saying, The Lord has done this to me in the days in which he looked on me to take away my reproach among men.

The birth of Jesus is foretold

In the sixth month the angel, Gabriel, was sent from God to a city in Galilee called Nazareth,

To a virgin espoused to a man whose name was Joseph, of the house of David, and the virgin's name was Mary.

And the angel came to her and said, Hail, you are highly favored, the Lord is with you, blessed are you among women.

And when she saw him, she was troubled at his saying and considered in her mind what manner of greeting this was.

And the angel said to her, Fear not, Mary, for you have found favor with God.

And you shall conceive in your womb and shall have a son, and his name will be Jesus.

Mary visits Elizabeth

Mary went into the hill country into a city of Judah and entered into the house of Zacharias and greeted Elizabeth.

And when Elizabeth heard the voice of Mary, the baby leaped in her womb, and Elizabeth was filled with the Holy Spirit.

And she spoke in a loud voice and said, Blessed are you among women and blessed is the fruit of your womb.

And why is this granted to me that the mother of my Lord should come to me?

For as soon as I heard your voice in my ears, the baby in my womb leaped for joy.

And blessed is she who believed that there would be a fulfillment of what was spoken to her by the Lord.

The birth of John the Baptist

Now Elizabeth's time came and she had her baby, and it was a boy.

And her neighbors and her cousins heard how the Lord had shown great mercy on her, and they rejoiced with her.

And on the eighth day, they came to circumcise the child, and they called him, Zacharias, after his father.

But his mother said, No, he shall be called John.

And they said to her, There is no one in your family called by that name.

And they made signs to his father, asking him what he should be called.

And Zacharias asked for a writing tablet and wrote, His name is John. And they all marveled.

And his mouth was opened immediately, and his tongue loosened, and he spoke and praised God.

And fear came on all that lived around them, and all

this was talked about in the hill country of Judea.

And all that heard this thought to themselves, What manner of child will this be!

Nothing is mentioned in the Bible about how Mary and Joseph came together to be man and wife, but the following excerpt from the Cayce readings fills in some of the details:

Q. In what manner was Joseph informed of his part in the birth of Jesus?

A. First by Mathias or Judah. Then as this did not coincide with his own feelings, first in a dream and then the direct voice.

And whenever [comes] the voice, this always is accompanied with odors as well as lights; and oft the description of the lights is the vision, see?

Q. Was he disturbed when Mary became with child while yet a virgin?

A. Owing to his natural surroundings and because of his advanced age to [in comparison with] that of the virgin when she was given; or as would be termed in the present, because of what people say. Yet when assured, you see, that this was the divine, not only by his brethren but by the voice and by those experiences, he knew. For you see . . . from the time of the first promise, while she was still yet in training from the choice, there was a period of some three to four years; yet when he went to claim her as the bride, at the period of—or between sixteen and seventeen— she was found with child.

Q. How old was Joseph at the time of the marriage?

A. Thirty-six.

Q. How old was Mary at the time of the marriage?

A. Sixteen.

Q. Were Mary and Joseph known to each other socially before the choosing for them to be man and wife?

A. As would be chosen in a lodge, not as ye would term of visitations; neither as only chosen by the sect or the families. In those periods in most of the Jewish families, the arrangements were made by the parents of the contracting parties, you see; while in this [case]—these [two] were not as contracting parties from their families. For Ann and her daughter were questioned as to belonging to any [family], you see! Then it was not a choice altogether as that they were appointed by the leaders of the sect or of the group or of the lodge or of the church . . .   5749-8

Joseph's vision

The story of Joseph's doubt and reassurance is told in the following passage from the Bible:

The birth of Jesus came about in this way: When his mother, Mary, was espoused to Joseph, before they came together, she was found with child of the Holy Spirit.

Then Joseph, being a just man and not wanting to make a public example of her, thought of divorcing her privately.

But while he thought on these things, an angel appeared to him in a dream, saying, Joseph, you are a son of David; don't be afraid to take Mary as your wife for that which is conceived in her is of the Holy Spirit.

And she shall have a son, and you shall call his name, Jesus, for he shall save his people from their sins.

Now all this was done, that it might be fulfilled which was spoken by the Lord through the prophet, saying,

A virgin shall be with child and shall have a son, and they shall call his name, Immanuel, which means, "God with us."

Then Joseph awoke from his sleep, and did as the angel told him, and took Mary as his wife,

And knew her not till she had her first-born son; and he called him, Jesus.

The birth of Jesus

In those days, there went out a decree from Caesar Augustus that all the world should be taxed.

And all went to be registered, everyone to his own city.

And Joseph left Nazareth in Galilee to go to the city of David, which is called Bethlehem (because he was of the house and lineage of David).

And so it was that, while they were there, Mary had her baby.

And she brought him forth and wrapped him in swaddling clothes and laid him in a manger, because there was no room for them in the inn.

And there were in the same country shepherds abiding in the field, keeping watch over their flock by night.

And an angel of the Lord came to them, and the glory of the Lord shone round about them; and they were very much afraid.

And the angel said to them, Fear not: for, behold, I bring to you good tidings of great joy, which shall be to all people.

For unto you is born this day in the city of David a Savior, who is Christ the Lord.

And this shall be a sign to you: You will find the babe wrapped in swaddling clothes and lying in a manger.

And suddenly there was with the angel a multitude

of the heavenly host, praising God and saying,

Glory to God in the highest, peace on earth, good will toward men.

And when the angels had gone away, the shepherds said to one another, Let us go into Bethlehem and see this thing which has come to pass, which the Lord has made known to us.

And they went in a hurry and found Mary and Joseph and the babe lying in a manger.

And when they had seen it, they told everyone what the angel had told them concerning this child.

And all they that heard it wondered about those things which the shepherds told them.

But Mary kept all these things and pondered them in her heart.

And the shepherds returned, glorifying and praising God for all the things that they had seen and heard.

Cayce beautifully describes the nativity scene in the following reading:

Yes, we have the information that has been indicated respecting some of the events surrounding the birth of Jesus, the son of Mary, in Bethlehem of Judea.

The purposes are well known, for which the journey was made in the period. The activities of Joseph are well known. The variation or difference in their ages is not so oft dwelt upon. Neither is there much indicated in sacred or profane history as to the preparation of the mother for that channel through which immaculate conception might take place. And this, the immaculate conception, is a stumblingstone to many worldly-wise.

The arrival was in the evening—not as counted

from the Roman time, nor that declared to Moses by God when the second passover was to be kept, nor that same time which was in common usage even in that land, but what would *now* represent January sixth.

The weather was cool, and there were crowds on the way. For, it was only a sabbath day's journey from Jerusalem. There were great crowds of people on the way from the hills of Judea.

The people were active in the occupations of the varied natures in that unusual land. Some were carpenters—as those of the house of Joseph, who had been delayed, even on the journey, by the condition of the Mother. Some in the group were helpers to Joseph—carpenters' helpers. Then there were shepherds, husbandmen, and the varied groups that had their small surroundings as necessitated by the conditions of the fields about Nazareth.

In the evening then, or at twilight, Joseph approached the Inn, that was filled with those who had also journeyed there on their way to be polled for the tax as imposed by the Romans upon the people of the land. For, those had been sent out who were to judge the abilities of the varied groups to be taxed. And each individual was required by the Roman law to be polled in the city of his birth.

Both Joseph and Mary were members of the sect called the Essenes; and thus they were questioned by those not only in the political but in the religious authority in the cities.

Then there was the answer by the inn keeper, "No room in the inn," especially for such an occasion. Laughter and jeers followed, at the sight of the elderly man with the beautiful girl, his wife, heavy with child.

Disappointments were written upon not only the face of Joseph but the inn keeper's daughter, as well as those of certain groups about the inn. For, many saw the possibilities of an unusual story that might be gained if the birth were to take place in the inn. Also there was consternation outside, among those who had heard that Joseph and Mary had arrived and were not given a room. They began to seek some place, some shelter.

For, remember, many of those—too—were of that questioned group; who had heard of that girl, that lovely wife of Joseph who had been chosen by the angels on the stair; who had heard of what had taken place in the hills where Elizabeth had gone, when there was the visit from the cousin—and as to those things which had also come to pass in her experience. Such stories were whispered from one to another.

Thus many joined in the search for some place. Necessity demanded that some place be sought—quickly. Then it was found, under the hill, in the stable—above which the shepherds were gathering their flocks into the fold.

There the Savior, the Child was born; who, through the will and the life manifested, became the Savior of the World—that channel through which those of old had been told that the promise would be fulfilled that was made to *Eve;* the arising again of another like unto Moses; and as given to David, the promise was not to depart from that channel. But lower and lower man's concept of needs had fallen.

Then—when hope seemed gone—the herald angels sang. The star appeared, that made the wonderment to the shepherds, that caused the awe and consternation to all of those about the Inn; some making fun, some smitten with conviction that those unkind things said must needs be readjusted in their relationships to things coming to pass.

All were in awe as the brightness of His star appeared and shone, as the music of the spheres brought that joyful choir, *"Peace on earth! Good will to men of good faith."*

All felt the vibrations and saw a great light— not only the shepherds above that stable but those in the Inn as well.

To be sure, those conditions were later to be dispelled by the doubters, who told the people that they had been overcome with wine or what not.

Just as the midnight hour came, there was the birth of the Master.

The daughter of the inn keeper was soon upon the scene, as was the mother of the daughter, and the shepherds that answered the cry—and had gone to see what was come to pass.

Those were the manners, and the ones present soon afterwards. For, through the period of purification the Mother remained there, not deeming it best to leave, though all forms of assistance were offered; not leaving until there was the circumcision and the presenting in the temple to the magi, to Anna and to Simeon.

Such were the surroundings at the period of the birth of Jesus. 5749-15

The visit of the Magi

After Jesus was born in Bethlehem of Judea in the days of Herod, the king, there came Wise Men from the east to Jerusalem.

And they said, Where is he that is born King of the Jews? For we have seen his star in the east and have come to worship him.

When Herod heard this, he was troubled and all Jerusalem with him.

And he gathered all the chief priests and scribes together and demanded of them where Christ would be born.

They told him, In Bethlehem of Judea, for it is written by the prophet; Bethlehem in the land of Judah is not the least among the cities in Judah, for out of it shall come a Governor that shall rule my people, Israel.

Then Herod privately inquired of the Wise Men when the star had appeared.

And he sent them to Bethlehem and said, Go and search diligently for the young child; and when you have found him, send word to me, so I may come and worship him also.

The Wise Men then departed, and the star which they saw in the east went before them, till it came and stood over where the young child was.

They came into the house and saw the young child with Mary, his mother, and fell down and worshiped him. Then they opened their treasures and presented gifts of gold, frankincense, and myrrh.

But God warned them in a dream that they should not return to Herod, so they departed into their own country another way.

Cayce explains the relationship of the Wise Men to Jesus in the following reading:

As indicated by the travels of the Master during the periods of preparation, the whole earth, the whole world looked for, sought the closer understanding. Hence through the efforts of the students of the various phases of experiences of man in the earth, as may be literally interpreted from the first chapters of Genesis, ye find that

those who subdued—not that were ruled by, but subdued the understandings of that in the earth—were considered, or were in the position of the wise, or the sages, or the ones that were holy; in body and mind, in accord with purposes.

Hence we find the Wise Men as those that were seekers for the truth, for this happening; and in and through the application of those forces—as ye would term today psychic—we find them coming to the place "where the child was." Or they were drawn as those that were giving the thanks for this Gift, this expression of a soul seeking to show wayward man back to God.

So they represent in the metaphysical sense the three phases of man's experience in materiality; gold, the material; frankincense, the ether or ethereal; myrrh, the healing force as brought with same; or body, mind, soul.

These were the positions then of the Wise Men in their relationship, or to put into the parlance of the day—they were the encouragement needed for the Mother and those that had nourished, that had cherished this event in the experience of mankind.

They came during the days of purification, but to be sure only after she was purified were they presented to the Child.

Q. *What relation did they have with the later travels of Jesus?*

A. As has just been indicated, they represented then the three phases of man's experience as well as the three phases of the teacher from Egypt, from Persia, from India.   5749-7

The baby Jesus in the temple

When eight days were accomplished for the circumcising of the child, he was called Jesus. The name was given him by the angel before he was conceived in the womb.

When the days of Mary's purification according to the law of Moses were accomplished, they brought him to Jerusalem to present him to the Lord,

And to offer a sacrifice according to that which is said in the law of the Lord, a pair of turtledoves or two young pigeons.

There was a man in Jerusalem whose name was Simeon, and he was righteous and devout and the Holy Spirit was upon him.

And it was revealed to him by the Holy Spirit that he should not see death before he had seen the Lord's Christ.

He came by the Spirit into the temple just as the parents brought Jesus into the temple to fulfill the custom of the law.

Simeon took him up in his arms and blessed God and said, Lord, now let your servant die in peace for I have seen your salvation which you have prepared for all the people, a light to lighten the Gentiles and the glory of your people, Israel.

Joseph and Mary marveled at the things which he said.

And Simeon blessed them and said to Mary, This child is set for the fall and rising again of many in Israel and for a sign which shall be spoken against, yes, a sword shall pierce through your own soul also, that the thoughts of many hearts may be revealed.

There was one Anna in the temple, a prophetess who was very old and a widow. But she served God with fastings and prayers night and day.

She also saw Jesus and gave thanks to the Lord and spoke of him to all those who looked for redemption in Jerusalem.

The flight into Egypt

An angel of the Lord appeared to Joseph in a dream and said, Arise and take the young child and his mother and flee into Egypt and stay there until I send you word, for Herod will try to kill him.

So he took Jesus and Mary by night and departed into Egypt and stayed there until Herod was dead that it might be fulfilled which was spoken by the Lord through the prophet, saying, Out of Egypt have I called my son.

When Herod saw that he was mocked by the Wise Men, he was very angry and sent his men forth to kill all the children in Bethlehem that were under two years old.

This fulfilled that which was spoken by Jeremiah, the prophet, when he said, In Ramah was there a voice heard, weeping and great mourning, Rachel weeping for her children and would not be comforted, because they are not.

Cayce describes the flight into Egypt in the following readings:

Thus this entity, Josie, was selected or chosen by those of the Brotherhood—sometimes called White Brotherhood in the present—as the handmaid or companion of Mary, Jesus and Joseph, in their flight into Egypt.

This began on a evening, and the journey—through portions of Palestine, from Nazareth to the borders of Egypt—was made only during the night.

Do not understand that there was only Joseph, Mary, Josie and the Child. For there were other groups that preceded and followed; that there might be the physical protection to that as had

been considered by these groups of people as the
fulfilling of the Promised One.
    . . . close to, what was then Alexandria.
                                          1010-17

    . . . dwelling by the brooks or the portions
where there were wells, in the upper portion of
the Egyptian land to which they fled.
    During those periods of the journey the entity
[Josie] ministered; and it was no mean distance
for a very young child, and a very young
mother . . .   1010-12

The return of Mary, Joseph, and Jesus from Egypt is
described in the following passages from the Bible:

    After Herod died, an angel appeared in a dream to
    Joseph in Egypt and said, Take the young child and
    his mother and go into the land of Israel for they are
    dead who sought the young child's life.
        So he took the young child and his mother and
    returned to Israel. But when he heard that Archelaus
    ruled in Judea in the place of his father, Herod, he was
    afraid to go there. And being warned in a dream by
    God, he went to Galilee instead.
        And settled in a city called Nazareth that it might
    be fulfilled which was spoken by the prophets, He
    shall be called a Nazarene.

The boy Jesus in the temple

    Every year Joseph and Mary went to Jerusalem to
    celebrate the feast of the passover.
        And when Jesus was twelve years old, they went to
    Jerusalem for the feast.
        When the feast was over, Jesus stayed behind in
    Jerusalem, but Joseph and Mary did not know this.

They thought he was with their kinsfolk or acquaintances and traveled a day's journey.

And when they could not find him, they turned back to Jerusalem to look for him.

After three days they found him in the temple, sitting in the middle of the teachers, both hearing them and asking them questions.

Everyone that heard him was amazed at his understanding and answers.

And when they saw him, they were astonished, and his mother said to him, Son, why have you done this to us? We were very worried about you.

And he said to them, Why did you worry about me? Don't you know that I must be about my Father's business?

But they did not understand what he meant by this.

So he went with them to Nazareth and was subject to them, and his mother kept all these things in her heart.

And Jesus increased in wisdom and stature and in favor with God and man.

Cayce tells us about Jesus' training as a child in the following readings:

Q. Can any more details be given as to the training of the Child?

A. Only those that covered that period from six years to about sixteen, which were in keeping with the tenets of the Brotherhood; as well as that training in the law—which was the Jewish or Mosaic law in that period. This was read, this was interpreted in accordance with those activities defined and outlined for the parents and the companions of the developing body. Remember and keep in mind, He was normal, He developed normally. Those about Him saw those character-

istics that may be anyone's who wholly puts the
trust in God! And to every parent might it not be
said, daily, dedicate thy life that thy offspring may
be called of God into service—to the glory of
God and to the honor of thy name!   1010-17

*Q. Was Jesus as a child also able to perform
miracles, as the Catholic Church claims, and was
He clairaudient, clairvoyant, and did He remember
His past incarnations? [The readings tell us Jesus
had past incarnations as Adam, Enoch,
Melchizedek, Joshua, Zend, and Joseph, among others.]*
A. Read the first chapter of John and you will
see. ["And the Word was made flesh, and dwelt
among us . . . "] As to the activities of the child—
the apparel brought more and more the influence which today would be called a lucky charm,
or a lucky chance; not as a consciousness. This
began (the consciousness) with the ministry from
that period when He sought the activities from
the entrance into the temple and disputing or
conversing with the rabbi at the age of twelve.
Thus the seeking for the study through the associations with the teachers at that period. 2067-7

As a child, Jesus was taught by the leader of the
Essenes, a woman Cayce calls Judy. When Jesus grew
older, He traveled to India, Persia, and Egypt to be
taught by the great teachers of the time.

*Q. Tell about Judy teaching Jesus, where and
what subjects she taught Him, and what subjects she
planned to have Him study abroad.*
A. The prophecies! Where? In her home.
When? During those periods from His twelfth
to His fifteenth-sixteenth year, when He went to

Persia and then to India. In Persia, when His father died. In India when John first went to Egypt—where Jesus joined him and both became the initiates in the pyramid or temple there.

Q. What subjects did Judy plan to have Him study abroad?

A. What you would today call astrology.

2067-11

Q Under whom did He study in India?
A. Kshjiar [?].
Q. Under whom in Persia?
A. Junner [?].
Q. In Egypt?
A. Zar [?].
Q. Outline the teachings which were received in India [also Persia and Egypt].

A. [In India] Those cleansings of the body as related to preparation for strength in the physical, as well as in the mental man. In the travels and in Persia, the unison of forces as related to those teachings of that given in those of Zu and Ra. In Egypt, that which had been the basis of all the teachings in those of the temple, and the after actions of the crucifying of self in relationships to ideals that made for the abilities of carrying on that called to be done.   5749-2

Jesus in Egypt

According to the Cayce readings, the Great Pyramid in Egypt is not a tomb, but a monument built to stand for all time by the survivors of the destruction of the continent of Atlantis. It was built as a temple, and it was in this temple that Jesus and John the Baptist were initiated into the White Brotherhood of the Essenes.

When the Great Pyramid was opened in the 1800s, no body was found in the sarcophagus or coffin. This empty sarcophagus symbolizes Jesus' victory over the grave, since He broke the life and death cycle with His resurrection.

Q. Please describe Jesus' education in Egypt in Essene schools of Alexandria and Heliopolis, naming some of His outstanding teachers and subjects studied.

A. Not in Alexandria—rather in Heliopolis, for the period of attaining to the priesthood, or the taking of the examinations there—as did John. One was in one class, one in the other . . .

Not as teachers, but as being *examined* by these; passing the tests there. These, as they have been since their establishing, were tests through which ones attained to that place of being accepted or rejected by the influences of the mystics as well as of the various groups or schools in other lands. For, as indicated oft through this channel [Cayce], the unifying of the teachings of many lands was brought together in Egypt; for that was the center from which there was to be the radial activity of influence in the earth—as indicated by the first establishing of those tests, or the recording of time as it has been, was and is to be—until the new cycle is begun.

Q. Please describe Jesus' initiations in Egypt, telling if the Gospel reference to "three days and nights in the grave or tomb," possibly in the shape of a cross, indicate a special initiation.

A. This is a portion of the initiation—it is a part of the passage through which . . . each soul is to attain in its development, as has the world through each period of their incarnation in the earth . . . the record of the earth through the passage through the tomb, or the pyramid, is that through which each entity, each soul, as an initiate must pass for the attaining to the releasing of same—as indicated by the empty tomb, which has *never* been filled, see? Only Jesus was able to break same, as it became that which indicated His fulfillment.

And there, as the initiate, He went out—for the passing through the initiation, by fulfilling—as indicated in the baptism in the Jordan . . . He passed from that activity into the wilderness to meet that which had been His undoing in the beginning.   2067-7

Jesus went out from John's baptism to the wilderness to meet and overcome Satan, who had been Jesus' undoing in the beginning when He was Adam. Satan had tricked Adam and caused death to enter into our consciousness, so it became Jesus' fulfillment to overcome both death and Satan.

All of this is symbolized in the Great Pyramid by the empty sarcophagus and the seven stones above it. The empty sarcophagus shows that there is no death or that the spirit survives death. The seven stones above the sarcophagus symbolize the raising of energy through the seven endocrine centers during meditation and prayer. This is how Jesus overcame death, by being attuned to the higher centers of consciousness. This is also how each soul in the earth can develop and ultimately overcome death.

Jesus overcame the world by attuning to the Christ Consciousness within.

Q. What is the meaning and significance of the words Jesus and Christ as should be understood and applied . . . ?

A. . . . Jesus is the man—the activity, the mind, the relationships that He bore to others. Yea, He was mindful of friends, He was sociable, He was loving, He was kind, He was gentle. He grew faint, He grew weak—and yet gained that strength that He has promised, in becoming the Christ, by fulfilling and overcoming the world! Ye are made strong—in body, in mind, in soul and purpose—by that power in Christ. The *power*, then, is in the Christ. The *pattern* is in Jesus. 2533-7

A physical description of Jesus

At this point we know how Jesus was trained as a child, seeking and learning from the Essenes and the great teachers of that period. But what did He look like? Few people are aware that in the archives of Rome there is a physical description of Jesus. It is contained in a report written during Jesus' lifetime by a Roman, Publius Lentulus, to the Emperor Tiberias. It reads as follows:

There has appeared in Palestine a man who is still living and whose power is extraordinary. He has the title given him of Great Prophet; his disciples call him the Son of God. He raises the dead and heals all sorts of diseases.

He is a tall, well-proportioned man, and there is an air of severity in his countenance which at once attracts the love and reverence of those who see him. His hair is the color of new wine from the roots to the ears, and thence to the shoulders it is curled and falls down to the lowest part of them. Upon the forehead, it parts in two after the manner of Nazarenes.

His forehead is flat and fair, his face without blemish or defect, and adorned with a graceful expression. His nose and mouth are very well proportioned, his beard is thick and the color of his hair. His eyes are gray and extremely lively.

In his reproofs, he is terrible, but in his exhortations and instructions, amiable and courteous. There is something wonderfully charming in this face with a mixture of gravity. He is never seen to laugh, but has been observed to weep [Cayce tells us Jesus did laugh and quite often]. He is very straight in stature, his hands large and spreading, his arms are very beautiful.

He talks little, but with a great quality and is the handsomest man in the world.

The above description agrees with the one contained in the Cayce readings:

> . . . a [picture of Jesus] as might be put on canvas [would] be entirely different from all these which have been depicted of the face, the body, the eyes, the cut of the chin and the lack entirely of the Jewish or Aryan profile. For these were clear, clean, ruddy, hair almost like that of David, a golden brown, yellow-red . . .   5354-1

The ministry of John the Baptist

In those days came John the Baptist preaching in the wilderness of Judea.

And he said, Repent, for the kingdom of heaven is at hand.

For this is he that was spoken of by the prophet, Isaiah, when he said, The voice of one crying in the wilderness, Prepare the way of the Lord, make his path straight.

John had a coat of camel's hair and a leather belt, and his food was locusts and wild honey.

He went to Jerusalem and all Judea, and all the region around the Jordan River, and baptized people in the Jordan confessing their sins.

But when he saw that many of the Pharisees and Sadducees had come to be baptized, he said to them, You vipers! Who warned you to flee from the wrath to come?

Bring forth the fruits of repentance, and don't think to yourselves, We are Abraham's children, for I say to you that God is able to raise children of Abraham from these stones.

The axe is laid to the root of the trees, and every tree that does not bring forth good fruit will be cut down and cast into the fire.

I baptize you with water to repent, but the one that comes after me is mightier than I am, and the latchet of his shoes I am not worthy to loosen. He will baptize you with the Holy Spirit and with fire.

His fan is in his hand, and he will purge his floor and gather his wheat into the granary and will burn up the chaff with unquenchable fire.

The baptism of Jesus

Jesus came from Galilee to the Jordan River to John to be baptized by him.

But John said, No, it is I who should be baptized by you, so why do you come to me?

Jesus said to him, Permit it to be so for it becomes us to fulfill all righteousness. So John consented to him.

And after Jesus was baptized, he came out of the water, and the heavens were opened up, and he saw the Spirit of God descending like a dove to alight on him.

And a voice came from heaven saying, This is my beloved Son in whom I am well pleased.

The temptation of Jesus

Then Jesus was led by the Spirit into the wilderness to be tested by the devil.

He fasted for forty days and forty nights and afterward he was very hungry.

And the tempter came to him and said, If you are the Son of God, command that these stones be made into loaves of bread.

Jesus answered and said, It is written that man does not live by bread alone, but by every word that comes out of the mouth of God.

Then the devil took him to the holy city and sat him on the pinnacle of the temple and said to him, If you are the Son of God, throw yourself down, for it is written: He shall give his angels charge concerning you, and their hands shall bear you up, lest you hit your foot against a stone.

Jesus said, It is also written, You shall not put the Lord God to the test.

Again the devil took him to a very high mountain and showed him all the kingdoms of the world and their glory.

And said to him, All of this will I give you, if you will fall down and worship me.

Jesus said to him, Begone, Satan, for it is written, You shall worship the Lord God, and him only shall you serve.

Then the devil left him, and angels came and ministered to him.

The beginning of Jesus' ministry

When Jesus heard that John was cast into prison, he departed into Galilee, and leaving Nazareth he came and stayed in Capernaum which is on the coast in the borders of Zebulun and Naphtali.

That it might be fulfilled which was spoken by Isaiah the prophet, when he said, The land of Zebulun and the land of Naphtali by the sea beyond the Jordan, Galilee of the nations; the people who sat in darkness saw a great light and to them who sat in the region and shadow of death, light sprang up.

From that time Jesus began to preach and to say, Repent, for the kingdom of heaven is at hand.

Jesus' first disciples

As Jesus walked by the Sea of Galilee, he saw two brothers, Simon who is called Peter, and Andrew, his brother, casting a net into the sea for they were fishermen.

And he said to them, Follow me and I will make you fishers of men.

And they left their nets and followed him.

Going on from there he saw two other brothers, James, the son of Zebedee, and John, his brother, in a boat with Zebedee, their father, mending their nets, and he called them.

And they left the boat and their father and followed him.

The wedding at Cana

On the third day there was a marriage in Cana of Galilee, and the mother of Jesus was there along with Jesus and his disciples.

After a while the wine ran out, and Mary said to Jesus, They have no wine.

And Jesus said to her, Woman, what does this have to do with me? My hour has not yet come.

Mary said to the servants, Whatever he tells you to do, do it.

And they brought six large jars of stone, and Jesus

said to them, Fill them with water. So they filled them up to the brim.

Then he said to them, Pour some out now, and take it to the governor of the feast. So they took it.

And when the ruler of the feast tasted the water that was made wine and did not know where it came from (even though the servants knew), he called the bridegroom and said to him, Every man at the beginning brings out his good wine and when men have drunk that, then he brings out his lesser quality wine. But you have kept the good wine till now.

This was the first of the miracles that Jesus did in Cana of Galilee, and this showed his glory; and his disciples believed in him.

The following is Cayce's description of the wedding at Cana:

A great deal of that leading to the experience [the wine miracle], to be sure, is being skipped over. For, that came about soon after the return of the Master from the Jordan, and His dwelling by the sea, His conversation with Peter—after Andrew had told Peter of the happenings at the Jordan; and there was the wedding in Cana of Galilee.

The girl was a relative of those close to the Mother of Jesus, who prepared the wedding feast—as was the custom in that period, and is yet among those of the Jewish faith who adhere to the traditions as well as custom of those people chosen as the channel because of their purpose with God.

The girl [Clana] to be wed was a daughter of the cousin of Mary, a daughter of a younger sister of Elizabeth, whose name was also Mary. And she was the one spoken of as "the other Mary,"

and not as some have supposed.

The customs required that there be a feast, which was composed of the roasted lamb with the herbs, the breads that had been prepared in the special ways as were the custom and tradition of those who followed close to the faith in Moses' law, Moses' custom, Moses' ordinances.

The families of Mary were present, as well as those of the groom.

The groom, in the name Roael, was among the sons of Zebedee; being an elder brother of James and John who later became the close friends and the closer followers of Jesus.

The Master, returning with those who were hangers-on, naturally sought to speak with His mother. Learning of this happening He, too, with the followers, were bid to remain at the feast.

Much wine also was part of the custom. The day was what ye would call June third. There were plenty of flowers and things of the field, yet only a part of those things needed. For, the custom called for more of the meats prepared with certain herbs, and wines.

The day had been fine; the evening was fair; the moon was full. This then brought the activities with the imbibing more and more of wine, more hilarity, and the dance—which was in the form of the circles that were a part of the customs, not only of that land then but that are in your own land now and then being revived.

With those activities, as indicated, the wine ran low. Remember, the sons of Zebedee were among those of the upper class, as would be termed; not the poorer ones. Thence the reason why Mary served or prepared for her relative the feast.

From those happenings that were a portion of

her experience upon their return from Egypt—
as to how the increase had come in the food when
they had been turned aside as they journeyed
back towards the Promised Land—Mary felt,
knew, was convinced within herself that here
again there might be such an experience, with
her Son returning as a man starting upon His
mission. For, what was the pronouncement to
the mother when Gabriel spoke to her? What
was the happening with Elizabeth when the
mother spoke to her?

This might be called a first period of test. For,
had He not just ten days ago sent Satan away,
and received ministry from the angels? This had
come to be known as hearsay. Hence the natural
questioning of the mother-love for the purposes;
this Son—strange in many ways had chosen, by
the dwelling in the wilderness for the forty days,
and then the returning to the lowly people, the
fishermen, about this country. It brought on the
questioning by the mother.   5749-15

Part Two

His Ministry

Jesus went about all Galilee teaching in their synagogues and preaching the gospel of the kingdom, and
healing all manner of sickness and all manner of
disease among the people.

His fame went throughout all Syria; and they
brought him all the sick people that had various
diseases, including those who were possessed with
demons, epileptics, and those who had palsy, and he
healed them.

Then great crowds of people followed him from
Galilee, Decapolis, Jerusalem, and from beyond the
Jordan River.

The Sermon on the Mount

Seeing the crowds, Jesus went up onto a mountain,
and when he had sat down, his disciples came to him,
and he taught them saying,

Blessed are the poor in spirit, for theirs is the
kingdom of heaven.

Blessed are they that mourn, for they shall be
comforted.

Blessed are the meek, for they shall inherit the earth.

Blessed are they who hunger and thirst after righteousness, for they shall be filled.

Blessed are the merciful, for they shall obtain
mercy.

Blessed are the pure in heart, for they shall see God.

Blessed are the peacemakers, for they shall be
called the children of God.

Blessed are they who are persecuted for righteousness' sake, for theirs is the kingdom of heaven.

Blessed are you when men shall revile you, and
persecute you, and lie about you, for my sake.

Rejoice and be glad, for great is your reward in
heaven, for so persecuted they the prophets who came
before you.

You are the salt of the earth, but if the salt has lost its flavor, with what shall it be salted? It is therefore good for nothing, but to be thrown out and stepped on by the feet of men.

You are the light of the world, a city that is set on a hill cannot be hidden.

Neither do men light a lamp and put it under a basket, but they put it on a table, and it gives light to everyone.

Let your light so shine before men, that they may see your good deeds, and glorify your Father who is in heaven.

Do not think that I have come to destroy the law, or the prophets; I have not come to destroy, but to fulfill.

For truly I say to you, till heaven and earth pass away, not one dot or dash shall pass from the law until all is fulfilled.

Anyone that shall break the least of these commandments and shall teach men so, he shall be called the least in the kingdom of heaven; but anyone that shall do and teach them, he shall be called great in the kingdom of heaven.

Except that your righteousness exceed the righteousness of the scribes and the Pharisees, you shall not enter into the kingdom of heaven.

You have heard it said that you shall not kill and anyone that kills shall be in danger of judgment,

But I say to you that anyone that is angry with his brother without cause shall be in danger of judgment, and anyone that insults his brother and calls him a fool shall be in danger of hellfire.

So if you bring your gift to the altar, and you remember that your brother has anything against you,

Leave your gift at the altar, and go your way, and first reconcile with your brother, and then come and offer your gift.

Agree with your enemy quickly while you are with him, so that he does not deliver you to the judge, and the judge deliver you to the officer, to be thrown into prison.

I say to you, you shall not leave that prison until you have paid the last penny.

You have heard it said, You shall not commit adultery, but I say that anyone that looks at a woman with lust has committed adultery already in his heart.

If your right eye offends you, pluck it out and throw it away, for it is better for you that one of your members should die and not that your whole body should be cast into hell.

If your right hand offends you, cut it off and throw it away, for it is better for you that one of your members should die and not that your whole body should be thrown into hell.

It has been said that anyone that wants to divorce his wife should give her a writing of divorcement,

But I say that anyone that shall divorce his wife, except for the cause of fornication, causes her to commit adultery, and anyone who marries her that is divorced commits adultery.

You have heard it said, You shall not lie, but shall perform what you have sworn to before God.

But I say, swear not at all, neither by heaven, for it is God's throne, nor by earth, for it is his footstool, neither by Jerusalem, for it is the city of the King. Neither swear by your head because you cannot make one hair white or black.

But let your speech be, yes, yes, or no, no, for anymore than this is evil.

You have heard it said, An eye for an eye and a tooth for a tooth,

But I say to you that you resist not evil, and if someone strikes you on the right cheek, then turn the other one to him also.

If any man sues you to take away your coat, then let him have your cloak also.

And if anyone compels you to go a mile, go two with him.

Give to those that ask you and those that wish to borrow from you.

You have heard it said, You shall love your neighbor and hate your enemy,

But I say to you, love your enemies, bless them that curse you, do good to them that hate you, and pray for them who despitefully use you and persecute you,

So you may be the sons of your Father who is in heaven, for he makes his sun to rise on the evil and the good, and he sends rain on the just and on the unjust.

For if you love only those who love you, what reward do you have? Do not even the tax collectors do the same?

If you greet your family only, what do you do more than others? Do not even the heathen so?

Be therefore perfect, even as your Father who is in heaven is perfect.

Take heed that you do not your alms before men, to be seen by them, otherwise you have no reward from your Father who is in heaven.

When you do your alms, do not sound a trumpet as the hypocrites do, in the synagogues and in the streets, that they may have glory from men. I say to you, They have their reward.

But when you do your alms, let not your left hand know what your right hand does,

That your alms may be done in secret, and your Father who sees in secret will reward you openly.

When you pray you shall not be like the hypocrites are, for they love to pray standing in the synagogues and at the street corner, so everyone will see them. I say to you, they have their reward.

But when you pray, do not use vain repetitions, as

the pagans do, for they think that they shall be heard because of their many repetitions.

Do not be like them, for your Father knows what things you have need of, before you ask him.

Pray in the following manner:

Our Father who art in heaven, Hallowed be thy name.

Thy kingdom come. Thy will be done, In earth, as it is in heaven.

Give us this day our daily bread.

And forgive us our debts, as we forgive our debtors.

And lead us not into temptation, but deliver us from evil.

For thine is the kingdom, and the power, and the glory, forever. Amen.

If you forgive men their debts, your heavenly Father will also forgive you,

But if you do not forgive men their debts, neither will your Father forgive your debts.

When you fast, do not act like the hypocrites with a sad face, for they disfigure their faces so that people will know that they are fasting. Truly, I say to you, They have their reward.

But when you fast, anoint your head and wash your face, so you will not appear to be fasting except to your Father who is in secret, and your Father who sees in secret will reward you openly.

Lay not up for yourselves treasures upon earth, where moth and rust corrupt, and where thieves break in and steal,

But lay up for yourselves treasures in heaven, where neither moth nor rust corrupts, and where thieves do not break in and steal.

For where your treasure is, there will your heart be also.

The lamp of the body is the eye; if, therefore, your eye is healthy, your whole body will be full of light.

But if your eye is evil, your whole body will be full of darkness. If, therefore, the light that is in you is darkness, how great is that darkness!

No one can serve two masters, for either he will hate the one and love the other, or else he will hold to the one and despise the other. You cannot serve God and money.

I say to you, be not anxious for your life, what you shall eat, or what you shall drink, or what you shall wear. Is not life more than food and the body more than clothes?

Observe the birds, for they plant not, neither do they reap, nor do they gather into barns, yet your heavenly Father feeds them. Are you not much better than they?

Can any of you, by being anxious, add one inch to your height?

And why are you anxious for clothes? Consider the lilies in the field, how they grow, they toil not, neither do they spin,

And yet I say to you that even Solomon in all his glory was not arrayed like one of these.

So if God so clothes the grass of the field, which today is, and tomorrow is thrown into the oven, shall he not much more clothe you, O ye of little faith?

Therefore be not anxious saying, What shall we eat? or What shall we drink? or What shall we wear?

For the Gentiles seek after all these things. And your heavenly Father knows that you need all these things.

But seek first the kingdom of God and his righteousness, and all these things shall be given to you.

Be not, therefore, anxious about tomorrow, for tomorrow will be anxious for things of itself. Sufficient to the day is its own trouble.

Judge not, that you be not judged.

For with what judgment you judge, you shall be judged, and with what measure you measure, it shall be measured to you again.

And why look upon the speck that is in your brother's eye and not consider the beam that is in your own eye?

How will you say to your brother, Let me pull the speck out of your eye, and yet a beam is in your own eye?

You hypocrite, first cast the beam out of your own eye, and then you shall see clearly to cast the speck out of your brother's eye.

Do not give that which is holy to the dogs, neither cast your pearls before swine, or they will trample them under their feet, and turn again and lacerate you.

Ask and it shall be given to you, seek and you will find, knock and it shall be opened for you,

For every one that asks receives, and he that seeks finds, and to him that knocks it shall be opened.

What man is there of you who, if his son asks for bread, will give him a stone?

Or if he asks for a fish, will give him a snake?

If you then, being evil, know how to give good gifts to your children, how much more shall your Father who is in heaven give good things to those that ask him?

Therefore, do unto others as you would have them do unto you, for this is the law and the prophets.

Enter in at the narrow gate, for wide is the gate and broad is the way that leads to destruction, and many go in that way,

Because narrow is the gate and hard is the way, which leads to life, and few people find it.

Beware of false prophets who come to you in sheep's clothing, but inside are ravening wolves.

You shall know them by their fruits. Do men gather

grapes of thorns or figs of thistles?

Every good tree brings forth good fruit, but a corrupt tree brings forth bad fruit.

Every tree that does not bring forth good fruit is cut down and thrown into the fire.

Therefore, by their fruits you will know them.

Not every one that says to me, Lord, Lord, shall enter into the kingdom of heaven, but he that does the will of my Father who is in heaven.

Many will say to me in that day, Lord, Lord, have we not prophesied in your name? And in your name have cast out demons? And in your name done many wonderful works?

And then will I say to them, I never knew you, leave me; you that work evil.

Anyone who hears these sayings of mine and does them, I will liken him to a wise man who built his house upon a rock.

And the rain descended, and the floods came, and the winds blew and beat upon that house, and it did not fall, for it was founded upon a rock.

And every one that hears these sayings of mine and does them not will be like the foolish man who built his house upon the sand.

And the rain descended, and the floods came, and the winds blew and beat upon that house, and it fell; and great was the fall of it.

And when Jesus had ended these sayings, the people were astonished at his doctrine,

For he taught them as one having authority and not as one of the scribes.

The people around Jesus

This might be a good point to describe the people around Jesus just to set the scene as far as His friends and family are concerned.

First, there were the Essenes, headed by a woman Cayce calls Judy, of which Jesus, His family, His kinsman, and John the Baptist were members.

Then there were His twelve apostles: Peter; Andrew; James, the son of Zebedee; John; Philip; Bartholomew; Thomas; Matthew; Simon; James, the son of Alpheus; Lebbeus, whose surname was Thaddeus; and Judas Iscariot.

Jesus' own family, according to Cayce, consisted of Joseph and Mary, and His brothers, James and Jude, and His sister, Ruth.

Among Jesus' closest friends were the family of Martha, Mary Magdalene, and Lazarus. They lived in what Cayce called "the little house in Bethany" around which many of the activities involving the Master revolved, including the raising of Lazarus from the dead. (In fact, the town of Bethany changed its name to El Lazaria after the Crucifixion and that has remained its name to this day.)

My favorite story about Jesus, however, involves a man who was a nonbeliever. He had heard all the stories about the miracles performed by Jesus, the healings, the amazing things that Jesus said, but he did not believe. Then one day he saw Jesus in a crowd of people, and he saw His eyes. That was all it took, just one look into Jesus' eyes and the man became a believer. What powerful eyes those must have been!

Jesus heals the sick

After Jesus came down from the mountain, large crowds of people followed him.

And a leper came and worshiped him and said, Lord, if you will, you can make me clean.

And Jesus put out his hand and touched him and

said, I will; Be clean. And immediately his leprosy was healed.

Then Jesus said to him, Do not tell anyone, but go your way and show yourself to the priest, and offer the gift that Moses commanded for a testimony to them.

Jesus went to Capernaum, and a Roman centurion came to him and said, Lord, my servant is at home very sick of palsy.

And Jesus said to him, I will come and heal him.

The centurion answered and said, Lord, I am not worthy that you should come under my roof, but speak the word only and my servant will be healed.

For I am a man of great authority, having soldiers under me, and I say to this man, Go, and he goes, and to another, Come, and he comes, and to my servant, Do this, and he does it.

When Jesus heard this, he marveled and said to the people with him, I say to you, I have not found so great a faith, no, not in Israel.

And I say to you that many will come from the east and west and will sit down with Abraham, Isaac, and Jacob in the kingdom of heaven,

But the sons of the kingdom will be thrown out into outer darkness, and there will be weeping and gnashing of teeth.

Then Jesus said to the centurion, Go your way, and as you have believed, so be it done to you. And his servant was healed that same hour.

Jesus heals Peter's mother-in-law

When Jesus came to Peter's house, he saw his wife's mother lying in bed with a fever.

And he touched her hand, and the fever left her, and she rose up and ministered to him.

At evening time people brought to him many that were possessed with demons, and he cast out the

spirits with his word and healed all that were sick,
    That the prophecies of Isaiah might be fulfilled
when he said, He himself took our infirmities and
bore our sicknesses.

Jesus tests His followers

When Jesus saw the great crowds of people around
him, he gave the command to depart to the other side.
    And a certain scribe came to him and said, Master,
I will follow you wherever you go.
    And Jesus said to him, The foxes have holes, and the
birds have nests, but the Son of man has nowhere to
lay his head.
    And another of his disciples said to him, Lord,
permit me first to go and bury my father.
    But Jesus said to him, Follow me, and let the dead
bury their dead.

Jesus calms the storm

Jesus got into a boat, and his disciples followed him.
    And there arose a great storm in the sea, so that the
boat was covered with waves, but Jesus was asleep.
    So his disciples came to him and woke him up and
said, Lord, save us or we will perish.
    And he said to them, Why are you fearful, O ye of
little faith? Then he got up and rebuked the winds and
the sea, and there was a great calm.
    But the men marveled, saying, What manner of
man is this that even the winds and the sea obey him?

Jesus casts out the demons

Jesus went to the country of the Gadarenes, and he
met two people possessed with demons, exceedingly
fierce, so that no one could pass that way.

And they cried out, saying, What have we to do with you, Jesus, Son of God? Did you come here to torment us before the time?

A good distance off from them was a herd of many swine feeding.

So the demons begged him, saying, If you cast us out, permit us to go away into the herd of swine.

And he said to them, Go. And when they came out, they went into the herd of swine; and the whole herd of swine ran violently down a steep place into the sea and died in the waters.

Then the keepers of the swine fled and went into the city and told everyone what had happened to the people who were possessed with the demons.

And the whole city came out to meet Jesus, and when they saw him, they begged him to depart from their borders.

Jesus heals a man of palsy

And Jesus entered into a boat and passed over and came into his own city.

And they brought him a man sick with the palsy lying on a bed, and Jesus, seeing their faith, said to the sick man, Son, be of good cheer, your sins are forgiven.

And some of the scribes said to themselves, This man is blaspheming.

Jesus, knowing their thoughts, said, Why are you thinking evil thoughts?

For which is easier to say, Your sins are forgiven, or to say, Rise up and walk?

But that you may know that the Son of man has power on earth to forgive sins, he said to the sick man, Rise up and take your bed and go into your house.

And he rose up and went into his house.

And when the crowd saw this, they marveled and

glorified God, who had given such power to men.

Jesus calls Matthew

And after Jesus left there, he saw a man named Matthew sitting at the tax office, and he said to him, Follow me. And Matthew got up and followed him.

And it came to pass, as Jesus sat eating in the house, many tax collectors and sinners came and sat down with him and his disciples.

And when the Pharisees saw this, they said to his disciples, Why does your Master eat with tax collectors and sinners?

But when Jesus heard this he said to them, They that are well do not need a physician, but they that are sick do.

But go and learn what that means, I will have mercy and not sacrifice, for I have come not to call the righteous, but the sinners to repentance.

Then the disciples of John came to him and said, Why do we and the Pharisees fast often, but your disciples do not?

And Jesus said to them, Can the sons of the bridechamber mourn as long as the bridegroom is with them? But the day will come when the bridegroom will be taken from them, and then they will fast.

The parable of the wineskins

No man puts a piece of new cloth on an old garment, for that which is put in to fill it up takes from the garment, and the tear is made worse.

Neither do men put new wine into old wineskins, else the wineskins break, and the wine runs out, and the wineskins perish; but they put new wine into new wineskins, and both are preserved.

Jesus heals two women

While he said these things to them, there came a certain ruler, who worshiped him, saying, My daughter is even now dead; but come and lay your hand on her, and she shall live.

And Jesus got up and followed him, and so did his disciples.

And a woman who had been diseased with an issue of blood for twelve years came behind him and touched the hem of his garment;

For she said to herself, If I may but touch his garment, I will be well.

But Jesus turned about, and when he saw her, he said, Daughter, be of good comfort; your faith has made you well. And the woman was made well from that hour.

And when Jesus came into the ruler's house and saw the musicians and the people making a noise,

He said to them, Depart, for the maid is not dead, but sleeping. And they laughed him to scorn.

But when the people were put out, he went in and took her by the hand, and the maid arose.

And the fame of this went abroad into all the land.

Jesus heals two blind men

And when Jesus departed from there, two blind men followed him, crying and saying, Son of David, have mercy on us.

And when he came to the house, the blind men came to him; and Jesus said to them, Do you believe that I am able to do this? They said to him, Yes, Lord.

Then he touched their eyes, saying, According to your faith be it to you.

And their eyes were opened, and Jesus strictly charged them, saying, See that no one knows it.

But when they left, they spread his fame abroad in all that country.

Jesus casts out a demon

They brought to Jesus a dumb man possessed with a demon.

And when the demon was cast out, the man spoke, and the people marveled, saying, It was never so seen in Israel.

But the Pharisees said, He casts out demons through the prince of the demons.

And Jesus went about all the cities and villages, teaching in their synagogues and preaching the gospel of the kingdom and healing every sickness and every disease among the people.

But when he saw the multitudes, he was moved with compassion for them, because they were faint and were scattered abroad, as sheep having no shepherd.

Then he said to his disciples, The harvest truly is plentiful, but the laborers are few.

Pray, therefore, that the Lord of the harvest will send forth laborers into his harvest.

The twelve apostles

And he called to himself twelve disciples, and he gave them power against unclean spirits, to cast them out, and to heal all manner of sickness and all manner of disease.

Now the names of the twelve apostles are these: the first, Simon, who is called Peter; and Andrew, his brother; James, the son of Zebedee; and John, his brother;

Philip and Bartholomew; Thomas and Matthew, the tax collector; James, the son of Alpheus; and

Lebbeus, whose surname was Thaddeus; Simon, the Canaanite; and Judas Iscariot, who also betrayed him.

These twelve Jesus sent forth and commanded them, saying, Go not into the way of the Gentiles, and do not enter into any city of the Samaritans;

But go, rather, to the lost sheep of the house of Israel.

And as you go, preach, saying, The kingdom of heaven is at hand.

Heal the sick, cleanse the lepers, raise the dead, cast out demons; freely you have received, freely give.

Provide neither gold, nor silver, nor copper in your purses,

Nor a bag for your journey, neither two coats, neither shoes, nor yet a staff; for the workman is worthy of his food.

And into whatever city or town you enter, inquire who in it is worthy, and stay there till you leave.

And when you come into a house, greet it.

And if the house is worthy, let your peace come upon it; but if it is not worthy, let your peace return to you.

And whoever shall not receive you, nor hear your words, when you leave that house or city, shake off the dust of your feet.

For I say to you, It shall be more tolerable for the land of Sodom and Gomorrah in the day of judgment, than for that city.

I send you out as sheep in the middle of wolves; be, therefore, wise as serpents and harmless as doves.

But beware of men, for they will deliver you up to the councils, and they will scourge you in their synagogues,

And you shall be brought before governors and kings for my sake, for a testimony against them and the Gentiles.

But when they deliver you up, be not anxious how

or what you shall speak; for it shall be given you in that same hour what you shall speak.

For it is not you that speaks, but the Spirit of your Father who speaks in you.

And the brother shall deliver up the brother to death, and the father the child; and the children shall rise up against their parents and cause them to be put to death.

And you shall be hated of all men for my name's sake, but he that endures to the end shall be saved.

But when they persecute you in this city, flee into another; for I say to you, You shall not have gone over the cities of Israel, till the Son of man comes.

The disciple is not above his teacher, nor the servant above his lord.

It is enough for the disciple that he be like his teacher, and the servant like his lord. If they have called the master of the house, Beelzebub, how much more shall they call them of his household?

Fear them not, therefore; for there is nothing covered that shall not be revealed; and hidden that shall not be known.

What I tell you in darkness, speak that in the light; and what you hear in the ear, proclaim that from the housetops.

And fear not them who kill the body, but are not able to kill the soul; but rather fear him who is able to destroy both soul and body in hell.

Are not two sparrows sold for a farthing? And not one of them shall fall to the ground without your Father.

But the very hairs of your head are all numbered.

Fear not, therefore; you are of more value than many sparrows.

Whoever, therefore, shall confess me before men, him will I confess also before my Father, who is in heaven.

But whoever shall deny me before men, him will I also deny before my Father, who is in heaven.

Think not that I came to send peace, but a sword.

For I came to set a man against his father, and the daughter against her mother, and the daughter-in-law against her mother-in-law.

And a man's foes shall be those of his own household.

He that loves his father or mother more than me is not worthy of me, and he that loves son or daughter more than me is not worthy of me.

And he that takes not his cross and follows me is not worthy of me.

He that finds his life shall lose it, and he that loses his life for my sake shall find it.

He that receives you receives me, and he that receives me receives him that sent me.

He that receives a prophet in the name of a prophet shall receive a prophet's reward, and he that receives a righteous man in the name of a righteous man shall receive a righteous man's reward.

And whoever gives a cup of cold water to one of these little ones in the name of a disciple, I say to you, he shall in no way lose his reward.

The seventy

In addition to the twelve apostles, Jesus appointed seventy others and sent them two by two into every city and place, where He Himself would go.

Jesus links John the Baptist with Elijah

In the following passage Jesus reveals that John the Baptist was the reincarnation of the prophet, Elijah:

When Jesus had ceased commanding his twelve disciples, he left there to teach and to preach in their cities.

Now, when John the Baptist had heard in the prison the works of Christ, he sent two of his disciples,

And said to him, Are you he that should come, or do we look for another?

Jesus answered and said to them, Go and show John again those things which you have seen and heard:

The blind see, the lame walk, the lepers are cleansed, the deaf hear, the dead are raised up, and the poor have the gospel preached to them.

And blessed is he who shall not be offended in me.

And as they left, Jesus began to say to the multitudes concerning John, What went you out into the wilderness to see? A reed shaken by the wind?

But what did you go out to see? A man clothed in soft raiment? Behold, those that wear soft clothing are in kings' houses.

But what did you go out to see? A prophet? Yes, I say to you, and more than a prophet.

For this is he of whom it is written, Behold, I send my messenger before your face, who shall prepare the way before you.

I say to you, Among those born of women there has not risen one greater than John the Baptist; notwithstanding, he that is least in the kingdom of heaven is greater than he.

And from the days of John the Baptist until now the kingdom of heaven suffered violence, and the violent took it by force.

For all the prophets and the law prophesied until John.

And if you will receive it, this is Elijah, who was to come.

He that has ears to hear, let him hear.

But to what shall I liken this generation? They are

like children sitting in the market place and calling their fellows,

And saying, We have piped to you, and you have not danced; we have mourned to you, and you have not lamented.

For John came neither eating nor drinking, and they said, He has a demon.

The Son of man came eating and drinking, and they said, Behold, a man who is a glutton and a drunkard, and a friend of the tax collectors and sinners. But wisdom is justified by her children.

Then he began to upbraid the cities in which most of his mighty works were done because they did not repent:

Woe to you, Chorazin! Woe to you, Bethsaida! For if the mighty works which were done in you had been done in Tyre and Sidon, they would have repented long ago in sackcloth and ashes.

But I say to you, It shall be more tolerable for Tyre and Sidon at the day of judgment than for you.

And you, Capernaum, which is exalted to heaven, shall be brought down to Hades; for if the mighty works which have been done in you had been done in Sodom, it would have remained until this day.

But I say to you, That it shall be more tolerable for the land of Sodom in the day of judgment than for you.

At that time Jesus answered and said, I thank you, Father, Lord of heaven and earth, because you have hidden these things from the wise and prudent and have revealed them to babes.

Even so, Father, for so it seemed good in your sight.

All things are delivered to me by my Father, and no man knows the Son, but the Father, and no man knows the Father, except the Son, and he to whom the Son will reveal.

Come to me, all you that labor and are heavy laden, and I will give you rest.

Take my yoke upon you and learn of me, for I am meek and lowly in heart, and you shall find rest for your souls.

For my yoke is easy, and my burden is light.

Jesus visits the Pharisee

And one of the Pharisees desired that Jesus would eat with him. And he went into the Pharisee's house and sat down to eat.

And a woman in the city, who was a sinner, when she heard that Jesus was eating in the Pharisee's house, brought an alabaster box of ointment,

And stood at his feet behind him weeping and began to wash his feet with her tears, and wipe them with her hair, and kissed his feet, and anointed them with the ointment.

Now when the Pharisee saw this, he thought to himself, This man, if he were a prophet, would have known who and what manner of woman this is that touches him, for she is a sinner.

And Jesus answered saying, Simon, I have something to say to you. And he said, Master, say on.

There was a certain creditor who had two debtors: the one owed five hundred denarii and the other fifty.

And when they had nothing to pay, he frankly forgave them both. Tell me, Which of them will love him most?

Simon answered and said, I suppose the one he forgave the most. And Jesus said to him, You have judged rightly.

And he turned to the woman and said to Simon, See this woman? I entered your house, and you gave me no water for my feet. But she has washed my feet with tears and wiped them with the hair of her head.

You gave me no kiss. But this woman, since the time I came in, has not ceased to kiss my feet.

You did not anoint my head with oil. But this woman has anointed my feet with ointment.

So I say to you, Her sins, which are many, are forgiven, for she loved much. But to whom little is forgiven, the same loves little.

And he said to her, Your sins are forgiven.

And those that were eating with him began to think to themselves, Who is this that forgives sins also?

And he said to the woman, Your faith has saved you, go in peace.

Jesus teaches about the sabbath

At that time Jesus went on the sabbath day through the corn, and his disciples were hungry and began to pluck the ears of corn and to eat.

But when the Pharisees saw this, they said to him, Your disciples do that which is not lawful to do upon the sabbath day.

But he said to them, Have you not read what David did when he was hungry and those that were with him,

How he entered into the house of God and ate the showbread which was not lawful for him to eat, neither for those who were with him, but only for the priests?

Or have you not read in the law how that on the sabbath days the priests in the temple profane the sabbath and are blameless?

But I say to you that in this place is one greater than the temple.

But if you had known what this means, I will have mercy and not sacrifice, you would not have condemned the guiltless.

For the Son of man is Lord even of the sabbath day.

Jesus heals on the sabbath

And when he left there, he went into their synagogue.

And there was a man whose hand was paralyzed. And they asked him, Is it lawful to heal on the sabbath days? That they might accuse him.

And he said to them, What man shall there be among you that shall have one sheep, and if it falls into a pit on the sabbath day will he not take hold of it and lift it out?

How much, then, is a man better than a sheep? Therefore, it is lawful to do good on the sabbath days.

Then he said to the man, Stretch forth your hand. And he stretched it forth, and it was made well like the other.

Then the Pharisees went out and held a council against him, how they might destroy him.

But when Jesus knew this, he left there, and large crowds of people followed him, and he healed them all,

And charged them that they should not make him known,

That it might be fulfilled which was spoken by Isaiah, the prophet, who said, Behold my servant whom I have chosen, my beloved, in whom my soul is well pleased; I will put my Spirit upon him, and he will show justice to the Gentiles.

He shall not strive, nor cry; neither shall any man hear his voice in the streets.

A bruised reed shall he not break, and smoking flax shall he not quench, till he sends forth justice to victory.

And in his name shall the Gentiles trust.

Then they brought to him a man possessed with a demon, blind and dumb; and he healed him, insomuch that the blind and dumb both spoke and saw.

And all the people were amazed and said, Is this not the son of David?

A house divided against itself

But when the Pharisees heard this, they said, This fellow does not cast out demons, but by Beelzebub, the prince of the demons.

And Jesus knew their thoughts and said to them, Every kingdom divided against itself is brought to desolation, and every city or house divided against itself shall not stand.

And if Satan cast out Satan, he is divided against himself; how then shall his kingdom stand?

And if I, by Beelzebub, cast out demons, by whom do your sons cast them out? Therefore, they shall be your judges.

But if I cast out demons by the Spirit of God, then the kingdom of God has come to you.

Or else how can one enter into a strong man's house and spoil his goods, except he first bind the strong man? And then he will spoil his house.

He that is not with me is against me, and he that gathers not with me scatters abroad.

Therefore, I say to you, All manner of sin and blasphemy shall be forgiven men, but the blasphemy against the Holy Spirit shall not be forgiven men.

And anyone who speaks a word against the Son of man, it shall be forgiven him, but anyone who speaks against the Holy Spirit, it shall not be forgiven him, neither in this age, nor in the age to come.

Either make the tree good and its fruit good, or else make the tree corrupt and its fruit corrupt, for the tree is known by its fruit.

O generation of vipers, how can you, being evil, speak good things? For out of the abundance of the heart the mouth speaks.

A good man out of the good treasure of the heart brings forth good things, and an evil man out of the evil treasure brings forth evil things.

But I say to you that every idle word that men shall speak, they shall give account of it in the day of judgment.

For by your words you shall be justified, and by your words you shall be condemned.

The Pharisees seek a sign

Then some of the scribes and Pharisees said to him, Master, we would see a sign from you.

But he answered and said to them, An evil and adulterous generation seeks a sign, and there shall be no sign given to it, but the sign of the prophet, Jonah.

For as Jonah was three days and three nights in the belly of the whale, so shall the Son of man be three days and three nights in the heart of the earth.

The men of Nineveh shall rise in judgment with this generation and shall condemn it, because they repented at the preaching of Jonah, and a greater than Jonah is here.

The queen of the south shall rise up in the judgment with this generation and shall condemn it, for she came from the farthest parts of the earth to hear the wisdom of Solomon, and a greater than Solomon is here.

When the unclean spirit is gone out of a man, he walks through the desert seeking rest and does not find it.

Then he says, I will return to my house from which I have come, and when he goes there he finds it empty, swept, and put in order.

Then he goes and takes with him seven other spirits more wicked than himself, and they enter in and stay there; and the last state of that man is worse than the first. So shall it be for this wicked generation.

Jesus' true brethren

While he was talking to the people, his mother and his brothers stood outside, desiring to speak with him.

Then someone said to him, Your mother and your brothers are standing outside, desiring to speak with you.

But he answered and said, Who is my mother? And who are my brothers?

And he stretched forth his hand toward his disciples and said, Behold my mother and my brothers!

For whoever shall do the will of my Father who is in heaven, the same is my brother and sister and mother.

Jesus teaches in parables

The same day Jesus went out of the house and sat by the seaside.

And great multitudes gathered around him, so that he got into a boat and sat, and the whole multitude stood on the shore.

And he said many things to them in parables, saying, A sower went forth to sow;

And when he sowed, some of the seeds fell by the wayside, and the birds came and ate them.

Some fell on stony places, where there was not much earth; and they sprang up, because they had no deepness of earth.

And when the sun came up, they were scorched, and because they had no root, they withered away.

And some fell among thorns, and the thorns sprang up and choked them.

But other seed fell into good ground and brought forth fruit, some a hundredfold, some sixtyfold, some thirtyfold.

Those who have ears to hear, let them hear.

And the disciples came and said to him, Why do you speak to them in parables?

He answered and said, Because it is given to you to know the mysteries of the kingdom of heaven, but to them it is not given.

For whoever has, to him shall be given, and he shall have more abundance; but whoever has not, from him shall be taken away even that which he has.

Therefore I speak to them in parables because they seeing, see not; and hearing, they hear not, neither do they understand.

And in them is fulfilled the prophecy of Isaiah which says, By hearing, you shall hear and shall not understand; and seeing, you shall see and shall not perceive.

For this people's heart has become hardened, and their ears are deaf, and their eyes are closed, lest at any time they should see with their eyes and hear with their ears and should understand with their heart and should be converted, and I should heal them.

But blessed are your eyes, for they see; and your ears, for they hear.

For I say to you that many prophets and righteous men have desired to see those things which you see and have not seen them; and to hear those things which you hear and have not heard them.

Hear, then, the parable of the sower.

When anyone hears the word of the kingdom and does not understand it, then the wicked one comes and takes away that which was sown in his heart. This is he which received seed by the wayside.

But he that received the seed in stony places, the same is he that hears the word and immediately with joy receives it;

Yet has he not root in himself, but endures for a while, then when tribulation or persecution arises because of the word, immediately he is offended.

He also that received seed among the thorns is he that hears the word, and the care of this age and the deceitfulness of riches choke the word, and he becomes unfruitful.

But he that received seed in the good ground is he that hears the word and understands it; who also bears fruit and brings forth, some a hundredfold, some sixty, some thirty.

He told them another parable, saying, The kingdom of heaven is like a man who sowed good seed in his field;

But while men slept, his enemy came and sowed weeds among the wheat and went his way.

But when the blades sprang up and brought forth fruit, then the weeds appeared also.

So the servants of the householder came and said to him, Didn't you sow good seed in your field? From where, then, has it weeds?

He said to them, An enemy has done this. The servants said to him, Do you want us to go and gather them up?

But he said, No; lest while you gather up the weeds, you root up the wheat also.

Let both grow together until the harvest; and at the time of the harvest I will say to the reapers, Gather together first the weeds and bind them in bundles to burn them, but gather the wheat into my barn.

Then he told them another parable, saying, The kingdom of heaven is like a grain of mustard seed which a man took and sowed in his field;

Which, indeed, is the least of all seeds; but when it is grown, it is the greatest among herbs and becomes a tree, so that the birds come and lodge in the branches of it.

Another parable he told them, saying, The kingdom of heaven is like leaven which a woman took and hid in three measures of meal, till the whole was leavened.

All these things Jesus told the multitude in parables, and he did not speak to them except in parables,

That it might be fulfilled which was spoken by the prophet, saying, I will open my mouth in parables; I will utter things which have been kept secret from the foundation of the world.

Then Jesus sent the multitude away and went into the house, and his disciples came to him and said, Explain to us the parable of the weeds of the field.

He answered and said to them, He that sows the good seed is the Son of man;

The field is the world, the good seed are the children of the kingdom, but the weeds are the children of the wicked one;

The enemy that sowed them is the devil, the harvest is the end of the age, and the reapers are the angels.

As, therefore, the weeds are gathered and burned in the fire, so shall it be at the end of this age.

The Son of man shall send forth his angels, and they shall gather out of his kingdom all things that offend and they that do evil,

And shall cast them into a furnace of fire; there shall be wailing and gnashing of teeth.

Then shall the righteous shine forth as the sun in the kingdom of their Father. Those who have ears to hear, let them hear.

The kingdom of heaven is like treasure hidden in a field, which when a man has found it, he hides it, and for the joy of it goes and sells all that he has and buys that field.

The kingdom of heaven is like a merchant seeking fine pearls,

Who, when he finds one of great price, goes and sells all that he has and buys it.

The kingdom of heaven is like a net that was cast into the sea and gathered every kind of fish,

Which, when it was full, they drew to shore and sat down and gathered the good into vessels, but threw the bad away.

So shall it be at the end of the age; the angels shall come forth and separate the wicked from among the righteous,

And shall throw them into the furnace of fire; there shall be wailing and gnashing of teeth.

Jesus said to them, Have you understood all these things? They said to him, Yes, Lord.

Then he said to them, Therefore, every scribe who is instructed concerning the kingdom of heaven is like a man that is a householder who brings forth out of his treasure things new and old.

A prophet in his own country

When Jesus had finished these parables, he departed from there.

And he came to Nazareth, where he had been brought up and, as was his custom, he went into the synagogue on the sabbath day and stood up to read.

And they gave him the book of the prophet, Isaiah. And he opened it and found the place where it was written,

The Spirit of the Lord is upon me, because he has anointed me to preach the gospel to the poor; he has sent me to heal the brokenhearted, to preach deliverance to the captives, to recover the sight of the blind, to liberate those that are bruised, and to preach the acceptable year of the Lord.

And he closed the book, and he gave it to the minister, and sat down. And all eyes were fixed on him.

And he said to them, This day is this scripture fulfilled in your ears.

And all bore him witness and wondered at the gracious words which proceeded out of his mouth. And they said, Is this not the carpenter's son? Is his mother not called Mary? And his brothers, James, and Joseph, and Simon, and Judas?

And his sisters, are they not all with us? From where, then, did this man get all these things?

And they were offended by him.

And he said to them, You will surely say to me the proverb, Physician, heal thyself; whatever we have heard done in Capernaum, do also here in your country.

And he said, A prophet is not without honor, except in his own country and in his own house.

But many widows were in Israel in the days of Elijah, when heaven was shut up three years and six months, when a great famine was throughout all the land;

But to none of them was Elijah sent, but only to Zarephath, a city of Sidon, to a woman that was a widow.

And many lepers were in Israel in the time of Elisha, the prophet; and none of them was cleansed, except for Naaman, the Syrian.

And the people in the synagogue, when they heard these things were filled with wrath,

And they rose up and threw him out of the city and led him onto the brow of the hill on which their city was built, so they might throw him off.

But he passed through the middle of them and went his way.

The murder of John the Baptist

At that time Herod Antipas, the son of Herod the Great, heard of the fame of Jesus,

And he said to his servants, This is John the Baptist; he is risen from the dead, and therefore mighty works do show forth themselves in him.

For Herod had laid hold on John and bound him and put him in prison for Herodias's sake, his brother Philip's wife.

For John had said to him, It is not lawful for you to have her.

And he would have put him to death, but he feared the multitude because they counted him as a prophet.

But when Herod had a birthday, the daughter of Herodias danced before them and pleased Herod.

So he promised with an oath to give her anything she would ask.

And she, being instructed by her mother to do so, said, Give me the head of John the Baptist on a platter.

And the king was sorry, nevertheless, for the oath's sake, and those who sat dining with him, he commanded it to be given to her.

And they went and beheaded John in the prison.

And his head was brought on a platter and given to the girl, and she brought it to her mother.

And his disciples came and took the body and buried it, and went and told Jesus.

When Jesus heard this, he left there by boat and went into the desert privately; and when the people heard of it, they followed him on foot out of the cities.

And Jesus went forth and saw a great multitude and was moved with compassion toward them, and he healed their sick.

The feeding of the five thousand

And when it was evening, his disciples came to him, saying, This is a desert, and the time is late; send the multitude away, so they may go to the villages and buy themselves food.

But Jesus said to them, They need not depart, feed them.

And they said to him, We have here but five loaves and two fishes.

He said, Bring them here to me.

And he commanded the multitude to sit down on the grass, and he took the five loaves and the two fishes and looking up to heaven, he blessed and broke and gave the loaves to his disciples, and the disciples gave them to the multitude.

And they all ate and were filled, and they took up the fragments that remained, twelve baskets full.

And they that had eaten were about five thousand men, besides women and children.

Jesus walks on the water

And Jesus told his disciples to get into a boat and to go before him to the other side, while he sent the multitudes away.

And when he had sent the multitudes away, he went up on a mountain privately to pray, and when the evening came, he was there alone.

But the boat was now in the middle of the sea, tossed by the waves, for the wind was blowing hard.

And in the fourth watch of the night Jesus came to them, walking on the sea.

And when the disciples saw him walking on the sea, they were troubled, saying, It is a ghost, and they cried out of fear.

But Jesus spoke to them, saying, Be of good cheer,

it is I; be not afraid.

And Peter answered him and said, Lord, if it is you, bid me to come to you on the water.

And He said, Come. And Peter came down out of the boat and walked on the water out to Jesus.

But when he saw the wind boisterous, he was afraid; and beginning to sink, he cried, Lord, save me.

And immediately Jesus stretched forth his hand and caught him and said to him, O ye of little faith, why did you doubt?

And when they came back to the boat, the wind ceased.

Then those that were in the boat came and worshiped him, saying, You are truly the Son of God.

And when they had passed over, they came into the land of Gennesaret.

And when the men of that place learned about him, they sent out into all the country round about and brought to him all that were sick,

And sought him that they might only touch the hem of his garment, and as many as touched were made perfectly well.

Then scribes and Pharisees from Jerusalem came to Jesus, saying, Why do your disciples transgress the tradition of the elders? For they do not wash their hands when they eat bread.

But he answered and said to them, Why do you also transgress the commandment of God by your tradition?

For God commanded, saying, Honor your father and mother, and He that curses father or mother, let him die.

But you say, Whoever shall say to his father or his mother, What you have gained from me is given to God, he need not honor his father.

So, for the sake of your tradition, you have made void the word of God.

You hypocrites, well did Isaiah prophesy of you, saying, This people draw near to me with their mouth and honor me with their lips, but their heart is far from me.

But in vain they worship me, teaching as doctrine the commandments of men.

And he called the multitude and said to them, Hear and understand:

It is not that which goes into the mouth that defiles a man, but that which comes out of the mouth, this defiles a man.

Then his disciples came and said to him, Did you know that the Pharisees were offended after they heard this saying?

But he answered and said, Every plant which my heavenly Father has not planted shall be rooted up.

Let them alone, they are blind leaders of the blind. And if the blind lead the blind, both shall fall into a ditch.

Then Peter said to him, Explain this parable to us.

And Jesus said, Are you also without understanding?

Do you not yet understand that what enters the mouth goes into the stomach and is cast out into the draught?

But those things which proceed out of the mouth come from the heart, and they defile the man.

For out of the heart proceed evil thoughts, murders, adulteries, fornications, thefts, lies, blasphemies.

These are the things which defile a man, but to eat with unwashed hands does not defile a man.

Then Jesus left there and went to the borders of Tyre and Sidon.

And a woman of Canaan came out of the same borders and cried to him, saying, O Lord, Son of David, my daughter is grievously vexed with a demon.

But he answered her not a word. And his disciples came and said to him, Send her away; for she cries after us.

And he answered and said, I am not sent but to the lost sheep of the house of Israel.

Then she came and worshiped him, saying, Lord, help me.

But he answered and said, It is not right to take the children's bread and to throw it to the dogs.

And she said, True, Lord, yet the dogs eat the crumbs which fall from their master's table.

Then Jesus said to her, Woman, great is your faith; be it so as you will. And her daughter was made well that very hour.

And Jesus left there and came near the Sea of Galilee and went up onto a mountain and sat down there.

And great multitudes came to him, having with them those that were lame, blind, dumb, maimed, and many others, and put them down at Jesus' feet, and he healed them,

So much so that the multitude wondered, when they saw the dumb to speak, the maimed to be well, the lame to walk, and the blind to see, and they glorified the God of Israel.

The four thousand are fed

Then Jesus called his disciples to him and said, I have compassion for the multitude because they have been with me now three days and have nothing to eat; and I will not send them away fasting, or they will faint in the way.

And his disciples said to him, From where should

we get so much bread in the wilderness as to feed so great a multitude?

And Jesus said to them, How many loaves do you have? And they said, Seven, and a few little fishes.

And he commanded the multitude to sit down on the ground.

And he took the seven loaves and the fishes and gave thanks and broke them and gave to his disciples and the disciples to the multitude.

And they all ate and were filled: and they took up of the broken pieces that were left seven baskets full.

And those that ate were four thousand men, besides women and children.

And he sent away the multitude and got into a boat and came into the land of Magadan.

The Pharisees and the Sadducees came and testing him, desired that he would show them a sign from heaven.

He answered and said, When it is evening, you say, It will be fair weather; for the sky is red.

And in the morning, It will be foul weather today, for the sky is red and overcast. O you hypocrites, you can discern the face of the sky, but you cannot discern the signs of the times?

A wicked and adulterous generation seeks a sign, and there shall be no sign given to it, but the sign of the prophet Jonah. And he left them.

And when his disciples came to the other side, they had forgotten to take bread.

Then Jesus said to them, Take heed and beware of the leaven of the Pharisees and of the Sadducees.

And they reasoned among themselves, saying, It is because we have taken no bread,

Which, when Jesus perceived, he said to them, O ye of little faith, why do you reason among yourselves, because you have brought no bread?

Do you not yet understand nor remember the five loaves of the five thousand and how many baskets you took up?

Nor the seven loaves of the four thousand and how many baskets you took up?

How is it that you do not understand that I spoke to you not about bread, but that you should beware of the leaven of the Pharisees and the Sadducees?

Then they understood that he warned them not to beware the leaven of bread, but to beware of the doctrine of the Pharisees and the Sadducees.

And he spoke a parable to them, saying, The ground of a certain rich man brought forth plentifully.

And he thought to himself, What shall I do, because I have no place to store my crops?

And he said, I will do this: I will pull down my barns and build a larger one, and I will store all my crops and my goods there.

And I will say to my soul, Soul, you have many goods laid up for many years; take it easy. Eat, drink, and be merry.

But God said to him, You fool, this night your soul shall be required of you; then whose shall these things be, which you have stored.

So he that lays up treasure for himself is not rich toward God.

Jesus reveals Himself as the Christ

When Jesus came to Caesarea Philippi, he asked his disciples, Who do men say that I, the Son of man, am?

And they said, Some say that you are John the Baptist; some, Elijah, and others, Jeremiah or one of the prophets.

He said to them, But who do you say that I am?

And Simon Peter answered and said, You are the Christ, the Son of the living God.

And Jesus answered and said to him, Blessed are you, Simon Barjona; for flesh and blood has not revealed this to you, but my Father who is in heaven.

And I say to you, That you are Peter and upon this rock I will build my church, and the gates of hell shall not prevail against it.

And I will give to you the keys of the kingdom of heaven, and whatever you shall bind on earth shall be bound in heaven, and whatever you shall loose on earth shall be loosed in heaven.

Then he told the disciples to tell no one that he was Jesus, the Christ.

From that time forward Jesus began to show his disciples how he must go to Jerusalem and suffer many things from the elders and chief priests and scribes and be killed and be raised again on the third day.

Then Peter took him and began to rebuke him, saying, God forbid, Lord, this will not happen to you!

But he turned and said to Peter, Get thee behind me, Satan. You are an offense to me; for you savor not the things that are of God, but those that are of men.

Then Jesus said to his disciples, If any man will follow me, let him deny himself, and take up his cross, and follow me.

For whoever will save his life shall lose it; and whoever will lose his life for my sake shall find it.

For what is a man profited, if he shall gain the whole world and lose his own soul? Or what shall a man give in exchange for his soul?

For the Son of man shall come in the glory of his Father with his angels, and then he shall reward every man according to his works.

Truly, I say to you, There are some standing here, who shall not taste death, till they see the Son of man coming in his kingdom.

* * *

And after six days Jesus took Peter, James, and John, his brother, and brought them to a high mountain privately,

And he was transfigured before them; and his face shone like the sun, and his raiment was as white as the light.

And, behold, there appeared to them Moses and Elijah talking with him.

Then answered Peter and said to Jesus, Lord, it is good for us to be here; if you will, let us make here three booths; one for you, one for Moses, and one for Elijah.

While he spoke, behold, a bright cloud overshadowed them, and behold, a voice out of the cloud said, This is my beloved Son, in whom I am well pleased; listen to him.

And when the disciples heard this, they fell on their faces and were very much afraid.

And Jesus came and touched them and said, Arise, and be not afraid.

And when they had lifted up their eyes, they saw no one except Jesus only.

Jesus links John the Baptist with Elijah

In the following passage Jesus again tells His disciples that John the Baptist was the reincarnation of Elijah:

And as they came down from the mountain, Jesus told them, Tell the vision to no one until the Son of man is raised again from the dead.

And his disciples asked him, Why do the scribes say that Elijah must come first?

And Jesus answered and said to them, Elijah truly shall come first and restore all things.

But I say to you, That Elijah has already come, and they knew him not, but have done to him whatever they desired. Likewise shall the Son of man also suffer from them.

Then the disciples understood that he spoke to them of John the Baptist.

* * *

And when they came to the multitude, there came to him a certain man, kneeling down and saying,

Lord, have mercy on my son, for he is epileptic and greatly vexed; for often he falls into the fire and often into the water.

And I brought him to your disciples, and they could not cure him.

Then Jesus answered and said, O faithless and perverse generation, how long shall I be with you? How long shall I bear with you? Bring him here to me.

And Jesus rebuked the demon, and he departed out of him; and the child was cured that very hour.

Then the disciples came to Jesus privately and said, Why couldn't we cast him out?

And Jesus said to them, Because of your unbelief; for I say to you, If you have faith as a grain of mustard seed, you shall say to this mountain, Move from here to there, and it shall move; and nothing shall be impossible for you.

But this kind of power comes only from prayer and fasting.

* * *

And while they were in Galilee, Jesus said to them, The Son of man shall be betrayed into the hands of men,

And they shall kill him, and on the third day he shall be raised again. And they were exceedingly sorry.

*   *   *

And when they came to Capernaum, those that received the tribute money came to Peter and said, Does your master pay tribute?

He said, Yes. And when he came into the house, Jesus spoke to him first, saying, What were you thinking, Simon? Of whom do the kings of the earth take custom or tribute? Of their own sons or of strangers?

Peter said to him, Of strangers. Jesus said to him, Then the sons are free.

Notwithstanding, lest we should offend them, go to the sea, and cast a hook, and take the first fish that comes up. And when you have opened its mouth, you shall find a coin; take it and give it to them for you and me.

Jesus and the Samaritan woman

Then Jesus came to a city of Samaria, which is called Sychar, near to the land that Jacob gave to his son, Joseph.

Now Jacob's well was there. Jesus, therefore, was tired from his journey and sat by the well, and it was late afternoon.

There came a woman of Samaria to draw water, and Jesus said to her, Give me a drink.

For his disciples had gone into the city to buy food.

And the woman of Samaria said to Jesus, How is it that you, being a Jew, asks for a drink from me, a woman of Samaria? For the Jews have no dealings with the Samaritans.

Jesus answered and said to her, If you knew the gift of God and who it is that asks you for a drink, you would have asked him, and he would have given you living water.

The woman said to him, Sir, you have nothing to draw with, and the well is deep, from where, then, have you this living water?

Are you greater than our father, Jacob, who gave us the well and drank from it himself, and his sons and his cattle?

Jesus answered and said to her, Whoever drinks of this water shall thirst again,

But whoever drinks of the water that I shall give him shall never thirst, but the water that I shall give him shall be in him a well of water springing up into everlasting life.

The woman said to him, Sir, give me this water, that I thirst not, nor come here to draw.

Jesus said to her, Go, call your husband and come here.

The woman answered and said, I have no husband. Jesus said to her, You have said well, I have no husband;

For you have had five husbands, and he whom you have now is not your husband, so you spoke truly.

The woman said to him, Sir, I perceive that you are a prophet.

Our fathers worshiped in this mountain, and you say that in Jerusalem is the place where men ought to worship.

Jesus said to her, Woman, believe me, the hour comes, when you shall neither in this mountain nor yet at Jerusalem worship the Father.

You worship you know not what. We know what we worship, for salvation is of the Jews.

But the hour comes and is now, when the true worshipers shall worship the Father in spirit and in truth, for the Father seeks such to worship him.

God is a Spirit, and they that worship him must worship him in spirit and in truth.

The woman said to him, I know that the Messiah

will come, who is called Christ, and when he comes, he will tell us all things.

Jesus said to her, I that speak to you am he.

And then his disciples came and marveled that he was talking with the woman. Yet no one said, What are you doing? or Why are you talking with this woman?

The woman then left her waterpot and went her way into the city and said to the men,

Come see this man who told me everything I have ever done. Is this not the Christ?

Then they went out of the city and came to him.

In the meantime his disciples said to him, Master, eat.

But he said to them, I have bread you know not of.

Therefore the disciples said to one another, Did anyone bring him something to eat?

Jesus said to them, My food is to do the will of him that sent me and to finish his work.

Do not say, There are yet four months and then comes the harvest? Behold, I say to you, Lift up your eyes, and look on the fields, for they are white already to harvest.

And he that reaps receives wages and gathers fruit to life eternal, that both he that sows and he that reaps may rejoice together.

And here is a true saying, One sows and another reaps.

I sent you to reap that on which you did no labor, other men labored, and you entered into their labors.

And many of the Samaritans of that city believed in him because of the testimony of the woman who told them, He told me everything that I have ever done.

So when the Samaritans came to him, they asked him to stay with them, and he stayed there two days.

And many more believed because of his own word,

And said to the woman, Now we believe, not

because of your saying, for we have heard him ourselves and know that this is indeed the Christ, the Savior of the world.

Jesus teaches Nicodemus

There was a man of the Pharisees named Nicodemus, a ruler of the Jews;

The same came to Jesus by night and said to him, Rabbi, we know that you are a teacher from God; for no one can do these miracles that you do except that God be with him.

Jesus answered and said, Truly, I say to you, Except a man be born again, he cannot see the kingdom of God.

Nicodemus said to him, How can a man be born when he is old? Can he enter his mother's womb a second time and be born?

Jesus answered, Truly, I say to you, Except a man be born of water and of the Spirit, he cannot enter into the kingdom of God.

That which is born of the flesh is flesh and that which is born of the Spirit is spirit.

Marvel not that I said to you, You must be born again.

The wind blows where it will, and you hear the sound of it, but you cannot tell where it came from and where it goes; so it is with every one that is born of the Spirit.

Nicodemus answered and said to him, How can these things be?

Jesus answered and said to him, You are a teacher of Israel, and you do not know these things?

Truly, I say to you, We speak that which we know and testify to that which we have seen; and you do not receive our witness.

If I have told you earthly things, and you do not

believe, how shall you believe, if I tell you heavenly things?

And no man has ascended up to heaven, but he that came down from heaven, even the Son of man who is in heaven.

And as Moses lifted up the serpent in the wilderness, even so must the Son of man be lifted up,

That whoever believes in him should not perish, but have eternal life.

For God so loved the world, that he gave his only begotten Son, that whoever believes in him should not perish, but have everlasting life.

For God sent his Son into the world not to condemn the world, but that the world through him might be saved.

He that believes in him is not condemned; but he that does not believe is condemned already, because he has not believed in the name of the only begotten Son of God.

And this is the condemnation, that light came into the world, and men loved darkness rather than light, because their deeds were evil.

For everyone that does evil hates the light and does not come to the light, lest his deeds should be reproved.

But he that does truth comes to the light, that his deeds may be made manifest, that they are wrought in God.

Jesus and the woman taken in adultery

Jesus went to the mount of Olives.

And early in the morning he went into the temple, and all the people came to him; and he sat down and taught them.

And the scribes and Pharisees brought him a woman taken in adultery and said to him, Master, this woman was taken in adultery, in the very act.

Now Moses, in the law, commanded us that such should be stoned; but what do you say?

They said this to test him, that they might accuse him. But Jesus stooped down and with his finger wrote on the ground, as though he had not heard them.

So when they continued asking him, he lifted himself up and said to them, He that is without sin among you, let him cast the first stone at her.

And again he stooped down and wrote on the ground.

And they who heard it, being convicted by their own conscience, went out one by one, beginning with the oldest, even to the last; and Jesus was left alone with the woman only.

When Jesus had lifted himself up and saw none but the woman, he said to her, Woman, where are your accusers? Has no man condemned you?

She said, No man, Lord. And Jesus said to her, Neither do I condemn you; go, and sin no more.

Cayce tells us that when Jesus wrote on the ground, He wrote things that made the woman's accusers aware of their own sins. Therefore, they could not accuse her because they also were guilty.

Then Jesus spoke to them again, saying, I am the light of the world; he that follows me shall not walk in darkness, but shall have the light of life.

The Pharisees, therefore, said to him, You bear witness of yourself; your witness is not true.

Jesus answered and said to them, Though I bear witness of myself, yet my witness is true; for I know from where I came and where I go; but you cannot tell from where I come and where I go.

You judge after the flesh, I judge no man.

And yet if I judge, my judgment is true; for I am not alone, but I and the Father that sent me.

It is also written in your law that the testimony of two men is true.

I am one that bear witness of myself, and the Father that sent me bears witness of me.

Then they said to him, Where is your father? Jesus answered, You neither know me nor my Father; if you had known me, you would have known my Father also.

Jesus spoke these words in the treasury, as he taught in the temple. And no one laid hands on him, for his hour had not yet come.

Then Jesus said again to them, I go my way, and you shall seek me and shall die in your sins; where I go you cannot come.

Then said the Jews, Will he kill himself? Because he said, Where I go, you cannot come.

And he said to them, You are from beneath; I am from above; you are of this world, I am not of this world.

I said, therefore, to you, that you shall die in your sins; for if you believe not that I am he, you shall die in your sins.

Then they said to him, Who are you? And Jesus said to them, Even the same that I said to you from the beginning.

I have many things to say and to judge of you, but he that sent me is true; and I speak to the world those things which I have heard of him.

They did not understand that he spoke to them of the Father.

Then Jesus said to them, When you have lifted up the Son of man, then shall you know that I am he and that I do nothing of myself; but as my Father has taught me, I speak these things.

And he that sent me is with me. The Father has not left me alone, for I do always those things that please him.

Then Jesus said to those Jews who believed in him, If you continue in my word, then you are my disciples indeed;

And you shall know the truth, and the truth shall make you free.

They answered him, We are Abraham's seed and were never in bondage to any man. How can you say then, You shall be made free?

Jesus answered them, Truly, I say to you, Whoever commits sin is the servant of sin.

And the servant abides not in the house forever, but the son abides ever.

If the Son, therefore, shall make you free, you shall be free indeed.

I know that you are Abraham's seed, but you seek to kill me, because my word has no place in you.

I speak that which I have seen with my Father, and you do that which you have seen with your father.

They answered and said to him, Abraham is our father. Jesus said to them, If you were Abraham's children, you would do the works of Abraham.

You do the deeds of your father. Then they said to him, We are not born of fornication; we have one Father, even God.

Jesus said to them, If God were your Father, you would love me; for I proceeded forth and came from God; neither came I of myself, but he sent me.

Why do you not understand my speech? Because you cannot hear my word.

You are of your father, the devil, and lusts of your father you will do. He was a murderer from the beginning and abode not in truth, because there is no truth in him. When he speaks a lie, he speaks of his own; for he is a liar, and the father of it.

And because I tell you the truth, you do not believe me.

Which of you convicts me of sin? And if I tell the

truth, why do you not believe me?

He that is of God hears God's words; you, therefore, hear them not, because you are not of God.

Then the Jews answered him and said, Are we not
right in saying that you are a Samaritan and have a
demon?

Jesus answered, I do not have a demon, but I honor
my Father, and you dishonor me.

And I seek not my own glory; there is one that seeks
and judges.

Truly, I say to you, If a man keep my saying, he shall
never see death.

Then the Jews said to him, Now we know you have
a demon. Abraham is dead, and the prophets, and you
say, If a man keep my saying, he shall never taste of death.

Are you greater than our father, Abraham, who is
dead? And the prophets are dead. Who do you claim
to be?

Jesus answered, If I honor myself, my honor is
nothing; it is my Father that honors me, of whom you
say that he is your God.

Yet you have not known him, but I know him. And
if I should say, I know him not, I shall be a liar like you,
but I know him and keep his saying.

Your father, Abraham, rejoiced to see my day, and
he saw it and was glad.

Then the Jews said to him, You are not even fifty
years old, and you have seen Abraham?

Jesus said to them, Truly, I say to you, Before
Abraham was, I am.

Then they took up stones to throw at him, but Jesus
hid himself and went out of the temple, going through
the middle of them, and so passed by.

And as Jesus passed by, he saw a man who was blind
from birth.

And his disciples asked him, Master, who sinned,

this man or his parents, that he was born blind?

Jesus answered, Neither has this man sinned, nor his parents, but that the works of God should be made manifest in him.

I must work the works of him that sent me, while it is day; the night comes, when no man can work.

As long as I am in the world, I am the light of the world.

When he had spoken, he spit on the ground and made clay of the spittle and anointed the eyes of the blind man with the clay,

And said to him, Go, wash in the pool of Siloam. He went his way, therefore, and washed and came seeing.

The neighbors who had seen him before when he was blind said, Is this not the man that sat and begged?

Some said, This is he; others said, He is like him; but he said, I am he.

Therefore they said to him, How were your eyes opened?

He answered and said, A man called Jesus made clay and anointed my eyes and said to me, Go to the pool of Siloam and wash; and I went and washed, and I received sight.

Then they said to him, Where is he? He said, I do not know.

They brought him to the Pharisees.

And it was the sabbath day when Jesus made the clay and opened his eyes.

Again the Pharisees asked him how he had received his sight. He said to them, He put clay on my eyes, and I washed and do see.

Therefore some of the Pharisees said, This man is not of God, because he does not keep the sabbath day. Others said, How can a man that is a sinner do such miracles? And there was a division among them.

They said to the blind man again, What do you say about him, since he has opened your eyes? He said, He is a prophet.

But the Jews did not believe that he had been blind
and received his sight, until they called the parents of
him that had received his sight.

And they asked them, Is this your son who you say
was born blind? How, then, does he now see?

His parents answered them and said, We know that
this is our son and that he was born blind;

But by what means he now sees, we know not; or
who has opened his eyes, we know not. He is of age,
ask him. He can speak for himself.

His parents said this because they feared the Jews;
for the Jews had agreed already that if any man
confessed that he was Christ, he would be put out of
the synagogue.

Therefore his parents said, He is of age, ask him.

Then again they called the man that was blind and
said to him, Give God the praise; we know that this
man is a sinner.

He answered and said, Whether he is a sinner or
not, I know not; one thing I know, that I was blind and
now I see.

Then they said to him again, What did he do to
you? How did he open your eyes?

He answered them, I have told you already, and you
did not hear; why would you hear it again? Will you
also be his disciples?

Then they reviled him and said, You are his disciple, but we are Moses' disciples.

We know that God spoke to Moses; as for this
fellow, we do not know where he is from.

The man answered and said to them, Why here is
a marvelous thing, that you do not know where he is
from, and yet he has opened my eyes.

Now we know that God hears not sinners; but if any
man is a worshiper of God and does his will, God
hears him.

Since the world began have you heard of any man

that opened the eyes of one that was born blind?

If this man were not of God, he could do nothing.

They answered and said to him, You were altogether born in sins, and now you teach us?

And they cast him out.

Jesus heard that they had cast him out, and when he found him, he said to him, Do you believe in the Son of God?

He answered and said, Who is he, Lord, that I might believe in him?

And Jesus said to him, You have both seen him, and it is he that talks with you.

And he said, Lord, I believe. And he worshiped him.

And Jesus said, For judgment I have come into this world that they who see not, might see; and that they who see, might be made blind.

And some of the Pharisees who were with him heard these words and said to him, Are we blind also?

Jesus said to them, If you were blind, you should have no sin. But now you say, We see. Therefore, your sin remains.

Jesus, the good shepherd

Jesus said, He that enters not by the door into the sheepfold, but climbs up some other way, the same is a thief and a robber.

But he that enters in by the door is the shepherd of the sheep.

To him the porter opens, and the sheep hear his voice, and he calls his own sheep by name and leads them out.

And when he puts out his own sheep, he goes before them, and the sheep follow him; for they know his voice.

And they will not follow a stranger, but will flee

from him; for they know not the voice of strangers.

This parable Jesus told them; but they did not understand what he said to them.

Then Jesus said to them again, I say to you, I am the door of the sheep.

All that ever came before me are thieves and robbers, but the sheep did not hear them.

I am the door; by me if any man enter in, he shall be saved and shall go in and out and find pasture.

The thief comes to steal and to kill and to destroy; I have come that they might have life and that they might have it more abundantly.

I am the good shepherd; the good shepherd gives his life for the sheep.

But he that is a hired hand and not the shepherd, whose own the sheep are not, sees the wolf coming and leaves the sheep and flees; and the wolf catches them and scatters the sheep.

The hired hand flees, because he is a hired hand and cares not for the sheep.

I am the good shepherd and know my sheep and am known of mine.

As the Father knows me, even so know I the Father; and I lay down my life for the sheep.

And other sheep I have that are not of this fold; them also I must bring, and they shall hear my voice; and there shall be one fold and one shepherd.

Therefore my Father loves me, because I lay down my life, that I might take it again.

No man takes it from me, but I lay it down myself. I have power to lay it down, and I have power to take it again. This commandment have I received from my Father.

There was a division therefore again among the Jews about these sayings.

And many of them said, He has a demon and is mad; why do you listen to him?

Others said, These are not the words of someone with a demon. Can a demon open the eyes of the blind?

*   *   *

It was the feast of the dedication in Jerusalem, and it was winter.

And Jesus walked in the temple in Solomon's porch.

Then came the Jews round about him and said to him, How long do you make us doubt? If you are the Christ, tell us plainly.

Jesus answered them, I told you, and you did not believe; the works that I do in my Father's name, they bear witness of me.

But you do not believe, because you are not my sheep, as I said to you.

My sheep hear my voice, and I know them, and they follow me.

And I give them eternal life; and they shall never perish, neither shall any man pluck them out of my hand.

My Father, who gave them to me, is greater than all, and no man is able to pluck them out of my Father's hand.

I and my Father are one.

Then the Jews took up stones again to stone him.

Jesus answered them, Many good works have I shown you from my Father; for which of those works do you stone me?

The Jews answered him, saying, For a good work we stone you not, but for blasphemy; and because you, being a man, make yourself God.

Jesus answered them, Is it not written in your law, I said, You are gods?

If he called them gods, to whom the word of God came, and the scripture cannot be broken,

Do you say of him whom the Father has sanctified

and sent into the world, You blaspheme; because I said, I am the Son of God?

If I do not the works of my Father, believe me not.

But if I do, though you do not believe me, believe the works, that you may know and believe that the Father is in me, and I in him.

Therefore, they sought again to take him; but he escaped, and went away again beyond the Jordan to the place where John first baptized, and there he stayed.

And many resorted to him and said, John did no miracles, but all the things that John spoke of this man were true.

And many believed in him there.

The good Samaritan

Now a certain lawyer tested Jesus, saying, Master, what shall I do to inherit eternal life?

He said to him, What is written in the law? How does it read?

And he answered and said, You shall love the Lord your God with all your heart and with all your soul and with all your strength and with all your mind; and your neighbor as yourself.

And he said to him, You have answered right; this do, and you shall live.

But he, desiring to justify himself, said to Jesus, And who is my neighbor?

And Jesus answered and said, A certain man went down from Jerusalem to Jericho and fell among thieves, who stripped him of his clothes and wounded him and left, leaving him half dead.

And by chance there came down a certain priest that way; and when he saw him, he passed by on the other side.

And likewise a Levite, when he was at the place, came and looked at him and passed by on the other side.

But a certain Samaritan, as he journeyed, came where he was; and when he saw him, he had compassion on him,

And went to him, and bound up his wounds, pouring in oil and wine, and set him on his own beast, and brought him to an inn, and took care of him.

And on the next day, when he departed, he took out two coins and gave them to the host and said to him, Take care of him; and whatever you spend more, when I come again, I will repay you.

Which, now, of these three, do you think, was neighbor to him that fell among the thieves?

And he said, He that showed mercy on him. Then Jesus said to him, Go, and do likewise.

Mary Magdalene and Martha

Now it came to pass, as they went, that Jesus entered into a certain village; and a certain woman, named Martha, received him into her house.

And she had a sister, called Mary, who also sat at Jesus' feet and heard his word.

But Martha was burdened about serving dinner and said, Lord, do you not care that my sister has left me to serve alone? Tell her to help me.

And Jesus answered and said to her, Martha, Martha, you are anxious and troubled about many things.

But one thing is needed, and Mary has chosen the better part, which shall not be taken away from her.

Jesus raises Lazarus from the dead

Now a certain man was sick, Lazarus, of Bethany, the town of Mary and her sister, Martha.

(It was that Mary who anointed the Lord with ointment and wiped his feet with her hair, whose brother Lazarus was sick.)

Therefore, his sisters sent a message to Jesus, saying, Lord, he whom you love is sick.

When Jesus heard this, he said, This sickness is not to death, but for the glory of God that the Son of God might be glorified by it.

Now Jesus loved Martha and her sister and Lazarus.

When he heard, therefore, that he was sick, he stayed two days still in the place where he was.

Then, after that, he said to his disciples, Let us go into Judea again.

His disciples said to him, Master, the Jews of late sought to stone you, and you want to go there again?

Jesus answered, Are there not twelve hours in the day? If any man walks in the day, he will not stumble, because he sees the light of this world.

But if a man walks at night, he stumbles, because there is no light in him.

He said these things; and after that he said this to them, Our friend Lazarus sleeps; but I go, that I may awaken him out of his sleep.

Then the disciples said, Lord, if he sleeps, he shall do well.

However, Jesus spoke of his death, but they thought that he had spoken of him taking a rest in sleep.

Then Jesus said to them plainly, Lazarus is dead.

And I am glad for your sakes that I was not there, to the intent you may believe; nevertheless, let us go to him.

Then said Thomas, who is called Didymus, to his fellow disciples, Let us go also that we may die with him.

Then when Jesus came, he found that he had lain in the grave four days already.

Now Bethany was near Jerusalem, about two miles off.

And many of the Jews came to Martha and Mary to comfort them concerning their brother.

Then Martha, as soon as she heard that Jesus was coming, went and met him; but Mary sat in the house.

Then said Martha to Jesus, Lord, if you had been here, my brother would not have died.

But I know that even now whatever you will ask of God, God will give it to you.

Jesus said to her, Your brother shall rise again.

Martha said to him, I know that he shall rise again in the resurrection at the last day.

Jesus said to her, I am the resurrection and the life; he that believes in me, though he were dead, yet shall he live.

And whoever lives and believes in me shall never die. Do you believe this?

She said to him, Yes, Lord, I believe that you are the Christ, the Son of God, who should come into the world.

And when she had said this, she went her way and called Mary, her sister, secretly, saying, The Master has come and calls for you.

As soon as she heard that, she rose quickly and came to him.

Now Jesus had not yet come into the town, but was in the place where Martha met him.

The Jews, then, who were with Mary in the house and comforted her, when they saw that she rose up quickly and went out, followed her, saying, She is going to the grave to weep.

Then, when Mary came to where Jesus was and saw him, she fell down at his feet and said to him, Lord, if you had been here, my brother would not have died.

When Jesus, therefore, saw her weeping, and the Jews also weeping who came with her, he groaned in the spirit, and was troubled,

And said, Where have you laid him? They said to him, Lord, come and see.

Jesus wept.

Then the Jews said, Behold how he loved him!

And some of them said, Couldn't this man, who opened the eyes of the blind, have saved Lazarus from dying?

Jesus, therefore, again groaning in himself, came to the grave. It was a cave, and a stone lay upon it.

Jesus said, Take away the stone. Martha, the sister of him that was dead, said to him, Lord, by this time he stinks; for he has been dead four days.

Jesus said to her, Said I not to you that, if you would believe, you should see the glory of God?

Then they took away the stone from the place where the dead was laid. And Jesus lifted up his eyes and said, Father, I thank you that you have heard me.

And I know that you hear me always; but because of the people who stand by I say this, that they may believe that you have sent me.

And when he had spoken, he cried with a loud voice, Lazarus, come forth.

And he that was dead came forth, bound hand and foot with graveclothes; and his face was bound about with a cloth. Jesus said to them, Loose him, and let him go.

Jesus teaches about the kingdom of heaven

At the same time the disciples came to Jesus and said, Who is the greatest in the kingdom of heaven?

And Jesus called a little child to him and sat him in the middle of them,

And said, I say to you, Except you be converted and become as little children, you shall not enter into the kingdom of heaven.

Whoever, therefore, shall humble himself as this little child, the same is the greatest in the kingdom of heaven.

And whoever shall receive one such little child in my name receives me.

But whoever shall offend one of these little ones who believe in me, it were better for him that a millstone were hanged about his neck and that he were drowned in the depth of the sea.

Woe to the world because of offenses! For offenses must come, but woe to the man by whom the offenses come!

Therefore, if your hand or your foot offends you, cut it off and cast it from you; it is better for you to enter into life lame or maimed, rather than, having two hands or two feet, to be cast into everlasting fire.

And if your eye offends you, pluck it out and cast it from you; it is better for you to enter into life with one eye, rather than, having two eyes, to be cast into hellfire.

Take heed that you despise not one of these little ones; for I say to you that in heaven their angels do always behold the face of my Father, who is in heaven.

For the Son of man comes to save that which was lost.

What do you think? If a man has a hundred sheep and one of them goes astray, does he not leave the ninety-nine and go into the mountains and seek the one that has gone astray?

And if he finds it, I say to you that he will rejoice more over that sheep than over the ninety-nine which did not go astray.

So it is not the will of your Father, who is in heaven, that one of these little ones should perish.

Moreover, if your brother sins against you, go and tell him his fault between you and him alone; if he shall hear you, you have gained your brother.

But if he will not hear you, then take with you one or two more, that in the mouth of two or three witnesses every word may be established.

And if he shall not hear them, tell it to the church; but if he shall not hear the church, let him be to you as a heathen man and a tax collector.

I say to you, Whatever you shall bind on earth shall be bound in heaven; and whatever you shall loose on earth shall be loosed in heaven.

Again I say to you that if two of you shall agree on earth as touching any thing that they shall ask, it shall be done for them by my Father, who is in heaven.

For where two or three are gathered together in my name, I am there also.

Jesus teaches forgiveness

Then Peter came to him and said, Lord, how often shall my brother sin against me and I forgive him? Till seven times?

Jesus said to him, I say not to you, Until seven times; but, Until seventy times seven.

Therefore is the kingdom of heaven like a certain king, who would take account of his servants.

And when he had begun to reckon, one was brought to him who owed him ten thousand talents.

But since he had nothing with which to pay, his lord commanded him to be sold, and his wife, and children, and all that he had, and payment to be made.

The servant, therefore, fell down and worshiped him, saying, Lord, have patience with me, and I will pay you all.

Then the lord of that servant was moved with compassion and released him and forgave him the debt.

But the same servant went out and found one of his fellow servants who owed him a hundred coins; and he laid hands on him and took him by the throat, saying, Pay me what you owe me.

And his fellow servant fell down at his feet and begged him, saying, Have patience with me, and I will pay you all.

And he would not, but went and threw him into

prison, till he could pay the debt.

So when his fellow servants saw what was done, they were very sorry and came and told their lord all that had happened.

Then his lord, after he had called him, said to him, You wicked servant, I forgave you all your debt, because you begged me to!

Shouldn't you have had compassion on your fellow servant, even as I had pity on you?

And his lord was angry and delivered him to the inquisitors, till he could pay all that was due.

So likewise shall my heavenly Father do to you, if you, from your hearts, do not forgive every one of your brother's sins.

Jesus teaches about divorce

When Jesus had finished these sayings, he left Galilee and came to Judea beyond the Jordan.

And great multitudes followed him, and he healed them there.

The Pharisees came to him also, testing him and saying to him, Is it lawful for a man to put away his wife for every cause?

And he answered and said to them, Have you not read that he who made them at the beginning, made them male and female;

And said, For this cause shall a man leave father and mother and shall cling to his wife, and they two shall be one flesh?

Therefore, they are no more two, but one flesh. What, therefore, God has joined together, let no man separate.

They said to him, Why did Moses then command to give a writing of divorcement and to put her away?

He said to them, Moses, because of the hardness of your hearts, permitted you to put away your wives, but from the beginning it was not so.

And I say to you, Whoever shall put away his wife, except it be for fornication, and shall marry another, commits adultery; and whoever marries her who is put away commits adultery.

His disciples said to him, If the case of the man be so with his wife, it is not good to marry.

But he said to them, All men cannot receive this saying, except they to whom it is given.

For there are some eunuchs, who were so born from their mother's womb; and there are some eunuchs, who were made eunuchs by men; and there are eunuchs, who have made themselves eunuchs for the kingdom of heaven's sake. He that is able to receive it, let him receive it.

Jesus blesses the little children

Then there were brought to him little children, that he should put his hands on them and pray, and the disciples rebuked them.

But Jesus said, Permit the little children, and do not forbid them to come to me; for such is the kingdom of heaven.

And he laid his hands on them and departed from there.

Jesus and the rich man

A man came to Jesus and said, Good Master, what good thing shall I do, that I may have eternal life?

And he said to him, Why do you call me good? There is none good but one, that is God; but if you will enter into life keep the commandments.

He said to him, Which? Jesus said, You shall not kill, You shall not commit adultery, You shall not steal, You shall not lie,

Honor your father and your mother, and You shall love your neighbor as yourself.

The young man said to him, All these things I have done from my youth. What do I lack?

Jesus said to him, If you will be perfect, go and sell what you have and give to the poor, and you shall have treasure in heaven, and come and follow me.

But when the young man heard this, he went away sorrowful, for he was very rich.

Then Jesus said to his disciples, I say to you that a rich man shall with difficulty enter into the kingdom of heaven.

And again I say to you, It is easier for a camel to go through the eye of a needle than for a rich man to enter into the kingdom of God. When his disciples heard this, they were amazed, saying, Who, then, can be saved?

But Jesus saw them and said to them, With men this is impossible, but with God all things are possible.

Then answered Peter and said to him, We have forsaken all and followed you. What shall we have, therefore?

And Jesus said to them, I say to you that you who have followed me, in the regeneration, when the Son of man shall sit on the throne of his glory, you also shall sit upon twelve thrones, judging the twelve tribes of Israel.

And every one that has forsaken houses, or brothers, or sisters, or father, or mother, or wife, or children, or lands, for my name's sake, shall receive a hundredfold and shall inherit everlasting life.

But many that are first shall be last, and the last shall be first.

The parable of the laborers

For the kingdom of heaven is like a man that is a

householder who went out early in the morning to hire laborers for his vineyard.

And when he had agreed with the laborers for a denarius a day, he sent them into his vineyard.

And he went out about the third hour and saw others standing idle in the market place,

And said to them, Go also into the vineyard, and whatever is right, I will give you. And they went their way.

Again he went out about the sixth and ninth hour, and did the same.

And about the eleventh hour he went out and found others standing idle and said to them, Go also into the vineyard, and whatever is right, that shall you receive.

So when evening came, the lord of the vineyard said to his steward, Call the laborers and give them their pay, beginning from the last to the first.

And when those that were hired about the eleventh hour came, they received every man a denarius.

But when the first came, they supposed that they should have received more, and they likewise received every man a denarius.

And when they had received it, they murmured against the householder, saying, These last have worked but one hour, and you have made them equal to us, who have borne the burden and the heat of the day.

But he answered one of them and said, Friend, I did you no wrong. Did you not agree with me for a denarius?

Take what is yours and go your way; I will give to the last, even as to you.

Is it not lawful for me to do what I will with my own? Is your eye evil, because I am good?

So the last shall be first, and the first last; for many are called, but few are chosen.

Jesus predicts His death and resurrection

And Jesus, going up to Jerusalem, took the twelve disciples aside along the way and said to them,

Behold, we go up to Jerusalem, and the Son of man shall be betrayed to the chief priests and to the scribes, and they shall condemn him to death,

And shall deliver him to the Gentiles to mock, and to scourge, and to crucify. And the third day he shall rise again.

Then the mother of Zebedee's children came to him with her sons, worshiping him, and desiring a certain thing of him.

And he said to her, What do you want? She said to him, Grant that these, my two sons, may sit, the one on your right hand and the other on the left, in your kingdom.

But Jesus answered and said, You do not know what you are asking. Are you able to drink of the cup that I shall drink of and to be baptized with the baptism that I am baptized with? They said to him, We are able.

And he said to them, You shall drink indeed of my cup and be baptized with the baptism that I am baptized with, but to sit on my right hand and on my left is not mine to give, but it shall be given to them for whom it is prepared by my Father.

And when the ten heard this, they were moved with indignation against the two brothers.

But Jesus called them to him and said, You know that the princes of the Gentiles exercise dominion over them, and they that are great exercise authority over them.

But it shall not be so among you, but whoever will be great among you, let him be your minister,

And whoever will be chief among you, let him be your servant;

Even as the Son of man came not to be ministered to, but to minister, and to give his life as a ransom for many.

Jesus and Zacchaeus

And Jesus entered and passed through Jericho.

And, behold, there was a man named Zacchaeus who was the chief among the tax collectors, and he was rich.

And he wanted to see Jesus, and he could not because of the crowd; for he was little of stature.

And he ran ahead and climbed up into a sycamore tree to see him, for he was to pass that way.

And when Jesus came to that place, he looked up and saw him and said to him, Zacchaeus, make haste and come down, for today I must stay at your house.

And he made haste and came down and received him joyfully.

And when they saw this, they all murmured, saying that he had gone to be the guest of a man that is a sinner.

And Zacchaeus stood and said to the Lord, Lord, I give half of my goods to the poor, and if I have taken anything from any man by false accusation, I restore to him fourfold.

And Jesus said to him, This day salvation has come to this house, since he is also a son of Abraham.

For the Son of man has come to seek and to save that which was lost.

And as they departed from Jericho, a great multitude followed him.

And two blind men sitting by the wayside, when they heard that Jesus was passing by, cried out, saying, Have mercy on us, Lord, Son of David.

And Jesus stood still and called them and said, What do you want me to do for you?

They said to him, Lord, open our eyes.

So Jesus had compassion on them and touched their eyes, and immediately their eyes received sight, and they followed him.

Part Three

The Resurrection
and
the Ascension

Jesus' triumphal entry into Jerusalem

And when they came near Jerusalem and had come to Bethphage, on the mount of Olives, then Jesus sent two disciples, saying to them, Go into the village opposite you, and straightway you will find a donkey tied and a colt with her; loose them and bring them to me.

And if anyone says anything to you, you shall say, The Lord has need of them, and straightway he will send them.

All this was done that it might be fulfilled which was spoken by the prophet, saying, Tell the daughter of Zion, Behold, your King comes to you, meek, and sitting upon a donkey, and a colt, the foal of a donkey.

And the disciples went and did as Jesus commanded them,

And brought the donkey, and the colt, and put on them their clothes, and sat him thereupon.

And a very great multitude spread their garments in the way; others cut down branches from the trees and spread them in the way.

And the multitudes that went before and that followed cried, saying, Hosanna to the Son of David! Blessed is he that comes in the name of the Lord! Hosanna in the highest!

And when he had come into Jerusalem, all the city was moved, saying, Who is this?

And the multitude said, This is Jesus, the prophet of Nazareth of Galilee.

Jesus drives the money-changers from the temple

And Jesus made a scourge of small cords, and went into the temple of God, and cast out all those that bought and sold in the temple, and overthrew the tables of the money-changers and the seats of those that sold doves,

And said to them, It is written, My house shall be a house of prayer, but you have made it a den of thieves.

And the blind and the lame came to him in the temple, and he healed them.

And when the chief priests and scribes saw the wonderful things that he did and the children crying in the temple and saying, Hosanna to the Son of David! they were very displeased.

And they said to him, Do you hear what they say? And Jesus said to them, Yes; have you never read, Out of the mouth of babes and sucklings you have perfected praise?

And he left them and went out of the city into Bethany, and he lodged there.

Now in the morning, as he returned to the city, he was hungry.

And when he saw a fig tree along the way, he came to it and found nothing on it but leaves only and said to it, Let no fruit grow on you from this moment on, forever. And the fig tree withered away!

And when the disciples saw this, they marveled, saying, How soon the fig tree withered away!

Jesus answered and said to them, Truly, I say to you, If you have faith and do not doubt, you shall not only do this to the fig tree, but also if you shall say to this mountain, Be gone and be cast into the sea, it shall be done.

And all things, whatever you ask in prayer, believing, you shall receive.

And when he had come into the temple, the chief priests and the elders of the people came to him as he was teaching and said, By what authority do you do these things? And who gave you this authority?

And Jesus answered and said to them, I also will ask you one thing, which, if you tell me, I likewise will tell you by what authority I do these things.

The baptism of John, from where did it come? From heaven or of men? And they thought to themselves, saying, If we say, From heaven; he will say to us, Why do you not then believe me?

But if we say, From men; we fear the people, for all hold John as a prophet.

And they answered Jesus and said, We cannot tell. And he said to them, Neither can I tell you by what authority I do these things.

Jesus teaches through parables

But what do you think? A certain man had two sons; and he came to the first and said, Son, go work today in my vineyard.

He answered and said, I will not, but afterward he repented and went.

And he came to the second and said the same. And he answered and said, I go, sir, and went not.

Which of the two did the will of his father? They said to him, The first. Jesus said to them, Truly I say to you that the tax collectors and the harlots go into the kingdom of God before you.

For John came to you in the way of righteousness, and you did not believe him, but the tax collectors and the harlots believed him; and you, when you had seen it, repented not afterward, that you might believe him.

Hear another parable: There was a certain householder, who planted a vineyard and hedged it round about and dug a winepress in it and built a tower and leased it to farmers and went into a far country.

And when the time of the fruit drew near, he sent his servants to the farmers, that they might receive the fruits of it.

And the farmers took his servants and beat one and killed another and stoned another.

Again, he sent other servants more than the first, and they did the same to them.

But last of all he sent to them his son, saying, They will revere my son.

But when the farmers saw the son, they said among themselves, This is the heir, come, let us kill him, and let us seize his inheritance.

And they caught him and threw him out of the vineyard and killed him.

When the lord, therefore, of the vineyard comes, what will he do to those farmers?

They said to him, He will destroy those wicked men and will lease his vineyard to other farmers, who shall give him the fruits in their seasons.

Jesus said to them, Did you never read in the scriptures, The stone which the builders rejected, the same will become the head of the corner; this is the Lord's doing, and it is marvelous in our eyes?

Therefore I say to you, The kingdom of God shall be taken from you and given to a nation bringing forth the fruits of it.

And whoever shall fall on this stone shall be broken, but on whoever it shall fall, it will grind him to powder.

And when the chief priests and Pharisees heard his parables, they perceived that he spoke of them.

But when they sought to lay hands on him, they feared the multitude, because they regarded him as a prophet.

And Jesus answered and spoke to them again in parables and said,

The kingdom of heaven is like a certain king, who made a marriage for his son,

And sent out his servants to call those that were

invited to the wedding; and they would not come.

Again, he sent out other servants, saying, Tell those who are invited, Behold, I have prepared my dinner, my oxen and my fatlings are killed, and all things are ready; come to the marriage.

But they made light of it and went their ways, one to his farm, another to his merchandise;

And the remnant took his servants and treated them shamefully and killed them.

But when the king heard of this, he was angry; and he sent out his armies and destroyed those murderers and burned up their city.

Then he said to his servants, The wedding is ready, but they who were invited were not worthy.

Go, therefore, into the highways and as many as you can find, invite to the marriage.

So those servants went out into the highways, and gathered together all, as many as they found, both bad and good; and the wedding was furnished with guests.

And when the king came in to see the guests, he saw a man who did not have a wedding garment on.

And he said to him, Friend, why did you come in here without a wedding garment? And he was speechless.

Then said the king to the servants, Bind him hand and foot and take him away and cast him into outer darkness; there shall be weeping and gnashing of teeth.

For many are called, but few are chosen.

Jesus addresses the Pharisees and the Sadducees

Then the Pharisees went and took counsel how they might entangle him in his talk.

And they sent out to him their disciples with the Herodians, saying, Master, we know that you are true and teach the way of God in truth, neither do you care for any man; for you regard not the person of men.

Tell us, therefore, What do you think? Is it lawful to give tribute to Caesar or not?

But Jesus perceived their wickedness and said, Why do you test me, you hypocrites?

Show me the tribute money. And they brought him a denarius.

And he said to them, Whose is this image and superscription?

They said to him, Caesar's. Then he said to them, Render, therefore, unto Caesar the things which are Caesar's, and unto God the things that are God's.

When they heard this, they marveled and left him and went their way.

The same day the Sadducees, who say that there is no resurrection, came to Jesus and asked him,

Saying, Master, Moses said, If a man dies having no children, his brother shall marry his wife and raise children for his brother.

Now there were with us seven brothers; and the first, when he had married a wife, died and, having no children, left his wife to his brother;

Likewise the second also, and the third, to the seventh.

And last of all the woman died also.

Therefore, in the resurrection whose wife shall she be of the seven? For they all had her.

Jesus answered and said to them, You do err, not knowing the scriptures nor the power of God.

For in the resurrection they neither marry nor are given in marriage, but are like the angels of God in heaven.

But concerning the resurrection of the dead, have you not read that which was spoken to you by God, saying,

I am the God of Abraham and the God of Isaac and the God of Jacob? God is not the God of the dead, but of the living.

And when the multitude heard this, they were astonished at his doctrine.

But when the Pharisees heard that he had silenced the Sadducees, they gathered together.

Then one of them, a lawyer, asked him a question, testing him and saying,

Master, which is the great commandment in the law?

Jesus said to him, You shall love the Lord, your God, with all your heart and with all your soul and with all your mind.

This is the first and great commandment.

And the second is like it, You shall love your neighbor as yourself.

On these two commandments hang all the law and the prophets.

While the Pharisees were gathered together, Jesus asked them, saying, What do you think of Christ? Whose son is he? They said to him, The Son of David.

He said to them, How, then, does David, in the Spirit, call him Lord, saying, The Lord said to my Lord, Sit on my right hand, till I make your enemies your footstool?

If David, then, calls him Lord, how is he his son? And no man was able to answer him a word, neither did any man from that day forward ask him any more questions.

Then Jesus spoke to the multitude and to his disciples, saying, The scribes and the Pharisees sit in Moses' seat.

All, therefore, whatever they ask you to observe,

observe and do; but do not after their works; for they say and do not.

For they bind heavy burdens grievous to be borne and lay them on men's shoulders, but they will not move them with one of their fingers.

But all their works they do to be seen by men; they make broad their phylacteries and enlarge the borders of their garments,

And love the uppermost places at feasts and the chief seats in the synagogues,

And greetings in the market places and to be called by men, Rabbi, Rabbi.

But be not called Rabbi, for one is your Master, Christ, and all are your brothers.

And call no one your father upon the earth; for one is your Father, who is in heaven.

Neither be called masters, for one is your Master, Christ.

But he that is greatest among you shall be your servant.

And whoever shall exalt himself shall be abased, and he that shall humble himself shall be exalted.

But woe to you, scribes and Pharisees, hypocrites! For you shut up the kingdom of heaven against men; for you neither go in nor permit them that are entering to go in.

Woe to you, scribes and Pharisees, hypocrites! For you devour widows' houses and for a pretense make long prayers, therefore, you shall receive the greater damnation.

Woe to you, scribes and Pharisees, hypocrites! For you compass sea and land to make one proselyte, and when he is made, you make him twofold more the child of hell than yourselves.

Woe to you, you blind guides who say, Whoever shall swear by the temple, it is nothing, but whoever shall swear by the gold of the temple, he is a debtor!

You fools and blind, for which is greater, the gold or the temple that sanctifies the gold?

And, Whoever shall swear by the altar, it is nothing; but whoever swears by the gift that is upon it, he is bound.

You fools and blind, for which is greater, the gift or the altar that sanctifies the gift?

Whoever, therefore, shall swear by the altar, swears by it and by all things on it.

And whoever shall swear by the temple, swears by it and by him that lives in it.

And he that shall swear by heaven, swears by the throne of God and by him who sits on it.

Woe to you, scribes and Pharisees, hypocrites! For you pay tithe of mint and anise and cummin, and have omitted the weightier things of the law, judgment, mercy, and faith; these you should have done and not to leave the other undone.

You blind guides, who strain at a gnat and swallow a camel.

Woe to you, scribes and Pharisees, hypocrites! For you make clean the outside of the cup and of the platter, but within they are full of extortion and excess.

You blind Pharisee, clean first that within the cup and platter, that the outside of them may be clean also.

Woe to you, scribes and Pharisees, hypocrites! For you are like whited tombs, which indeed appear beautiful outward, but are within full of dead bones and of all uncleanness.

You also appear outwardly righteous to men, but within you are full of hypocrisy and iniquity.

Woe to you, scribes and Pharisees, hypocrites! Because you build the tombs of the prophets and garnish the sepulchers of the righteous and say, If we had been in the days of our fathers, we would not have been partakers with them in the blood of the prophets.

Therefore, you are witnesses against yourselves, that you are the sons of them who killed the prophets.

Fill up, then, the measure of your fathers.

You serpents, you generation of vipers, how can you escape the damnation of hell?

Therefore, behold, I send to you prophets and wise men and scribes; and some of them you shall kill and crucify, and some of them shall you scourge in your synagogues and persecute them from city to city,

That upon you may come all the righteous blood shed upon the earth, from the blood of righteous Abel to the blood of Zechariah, son of Barachiah, whom you killed between the temple and the altar.

I say to you, All these things shall come upon this generation.

O Jerusalem, Jerusalem, that killed the prophets and stoned those who were sent to you, how often would I have gathered your children together, even as a hen gathers her chickens under her wings, and you would not!

For I say to you, You shall not see me again until you shall say, Blessed is he that comes in the name of the Lord.

Jesus predicts His return to earth

In the following passage Jesus outlines the events which will precede His return to earth:

And Jesus went out and left the temple, and his disciples came to him to show him the buildings of the temple.

And Jesus said to them, Do you see all these things? I say to you, There shall not be left here one stone upon another, that shall not be thrown down.

And as he sat upon the mount of Olives, the

disciples came to him privately, saying, Tell us, when shall these things be? And what shall be the sign of your coming and of the end of the age?

And Jesus answered and said to them, Take heed that no man deceive you.

For many shall come in my name, saying, I am Christ, and shall deceive many.

And you shall hear of wars and rumors of wars, see that you are not troubled; for all these things must happen, but the end is not yet.

For nation shall rise against nation and kingdom against kingdom, and there shall be famines and pestilences and earthquakes in diverse places.

All these are the beginning of sorrows.

Then shall they deliver you up to be afflicted and shall kill you, and you shall be hated of all nations for my name's sake.

And then shall many be offended and shall betray one another and shall hate one another.

And many false prophets shall rise and shall deceive many.

And because iniquity shall abound, the love of many shall grow cold.

But he that endures to the end, the same shall be saved.

And this gospel of the kingdom shall be preached in all the world for a witness to all nations; and then shall the end come.

When you, therefore, see the abomination of desolation, spoken of by Daniel the prophet, standing in the holy place (whoever reads, let him understand),

Then let them who are in Judea flee into the mountains,

Let him who is on the housetop not come down to take anything out of his house,

Neither let him who is in the field return back to take his clothes.

And woe to those who are with child and to those who nurse children in those days!

But pray that your flight is not in the winter, nor on the sabbath day;

For then shall be great tribulation, such as was not since the beginning of the world to this time, no, nor ever shall be.

And except those days should be shortened, there should no flesh be saved, but for the elect's sake those days shall be shortened.

Then if any man shall say to you, Lo, here is Christ, or there; believe it not.

For there shall arise false Christs and false prophets and shall show great signs and wonders, so much so that, if it were possible, they shall deceive the very elect.

Behold, I have told you before.

Therefore, if they shall say to you, Behold, he is in the desert; do not go forth; behold, he is in the secret chambers, do not believe it.

For as the lightning comes out of the east and shines to the west, so shall the coming of the Son of man be.

For wherever the carcass is, there will the eagles be gathered together.

Immediately after the tribulation of those days shall the sun be darkened, and the moon shall not give its light, and the stars shall fall from heaven, and the powers of the heavens shall be shaken.

And then shall appear the sign of the Son of man in heaven, and then shall all the tribes of the earth mourn, and they shall see the Son of man coming in the clouds of heaven with power and great glory.

And he shall send his angels with a great sound of a trumpet, and they shall gather together his elect from the four winds, from one end of heaven to the other.

Now learn the parable of the fig tree: When its

branch is tender and puts out leaves, you know that summer is near;

So likewise you, when you see all these things, know that it is near, even at the doors.

I say to you, This generation shall not pass, till all these things be fulfilled.

Heaven and earth shall pass away, but my words shall not pass away.

But of that day and hour knows no man, no, not the angels of heaven, but my Father only.

But as the days of Noah were, so shall the coming of the Son of man be.

For as in the days that were before the flood they were eating and drinking, marrying and giving in marriage, until the day that Noah entered into the ark,

And they did not know until the flood came and took them all away, so shall the coming of the Son of man be.

Then shall two be in the field, the one shall be taken and the other left.

Two women shall be grinding at the mill; the one shall be taken and the other left.

Watch, therefore, for you do not know in what hour your Lord comes.

But know this, that if the householder had known in what hour the thief would come, he would have watched and would not have allowed his house to be broken into.

Therefore be ready, for in such an hour as you think not, the Son of man will come.

Who, then, is a faithful and wise servant, whom his lord has made ruler over his household, to give them food in due season?

Blessed is that servant, who his lord, when he comes, shall find him so doing.

I say to you that he shall make him ruler over all his goods.

But if that evil servant shall say in his heart, My lord delays his coming;

And shall begin to strike his fellow servants and to eat and drink with the drunkards,

The lord of that servant shall come in a day when he is not looking and in an hour that he is not aware of,

And shall punish him and put him with the hypocrites, and there shall be weeping and gnashing of teeth.

Then the kingdom is like ten virgins, who took their lamps and went forth to meet the bridegroom.

And five of them were wise, and five were foolish.

They that were foolish took their lamps and took no oil with them;

But the wise took oil in their vessels with their lamps.

While the bridegroom delayed, they all slumbered and slept.

And at midnight there was a cry made, Behold, the bridegroom comes, go out to meet him.

Then all those virgins arose and trimmed their lamps.

And the foolish said to the wise, Give us some of your oil, for our lamps have gone out.

But the wise answered, saying, No, lest there not be enough for us and you; but go to them that sell and buy for yourselves.

And while they had gone to buy, the bridegroom came, and they that were ready went in with him to the marriage feast, and the door was shut.

Afterward the other virgins came, saying, Lord, Lord, open to us.

But he answered and said, Truly, I say to you, I know you not.

Watch, therefore, for you know neither the day nor the hour in which the Son of man comes.

For the kingdom of heaven is like a man traveling

into a far country, who called his servants and delivered to them his goods.

And to one he gave five talents, to another two, and to another one, to every man according to his ability, and straightaway took his journey.

Then he that had received the five talents went and traded with the same and made five talents more,

And likewise he that had received two, he also gained two more.

But he that had received one went and dug in the earth and hid his lord's money.

After a long time the lord of those servants came and reckoned with them.

And he that had received five talents came and brought the other five talents, saying, Lord, you gave me five talents, and, behold, I have gained five talents more.

His lord said to him, Well done, good and faithful servant, you have been faithful over a few things, I will make you ruler over many things. Enter into the joy of your lord.

He that had received two talents came and said, Lord, you gave me two talents; behold, I have gained two more talents beside them.

His lord said to him, Well done, good and faithful servant; you have been faithful over a few things, I will make you ruler over many things. Enter into the joy of your lord.

Then he that had received the one talent came and said, Lord, I knew you, that you are a hard man, reaping where you have not sown and gathering where you have not spread,

And I was afraid and went and hid your talent in the earth; lo, you have what is yours.

His lord answered and said to him, You wicked and slothful servant, you knew that I reap where I sowed not and gather where I have not spread?

You should, therefore, have given my money to the exchangers, and then, at my coming, I would have received mine own with interest.

Take, therefore, the talent from him and give it to him who has ten talents.

For to every one that has shall be given, and he shall have abundance, but from him that has not shall be taken away even that which he has.

And cast the unprofitable servant into outer darkness; there shall be weeping and gnashing of teeth.

When the Son of man comes in his glory and all the holy angels with him, then he shall sit upon the throne of his glory.

And before him shall be gathered all the nations; and he shall separate them one from another, as a shepherd divides his sheep from the goats.

And he shall set the sheep on his right hand, but the goats on the left.

Then shall the King say to them on his right hand, Come, you blessed of my Father, inherit the kingdom prepared for you from the foundation of the world;

For I was hungry, and you gave me food; I was thirsty, and you gave me water; I was a stranger, and you took me in;

Naked, and you clothed me; I was sick, and you visited me; I was in prison, and you came to me.

Then shall the righteous answer him, saying, Lord, when saw we you hungry, and fed you; or thirsty, and gave you water?

When saw we you a stranger, and took you in; or naked, and clothed you?

Or when saw we you sick, or in prison, and came to you?

And the King shall answer and say to them, I say to you, Inasmuch as you have done to the least of these, my brothers, you have done to me.

Then shall he say to them on the left hand, Depart

from me, you cursed, into everlasting fire, prepared for the devil and his angels;

For I was hungry, and you gave me no food; I was thirsty, and you gave me no water;

I was a stranger, and you did not take me in; naked, and you did not cloth me; sick and in prison, and you did not visit me.

Then they shall answer him, saying, Lord, when saw we you hungry, or thirsty, or a stranger, or naked, or sick, or in prison, and did not minister to you?

Then shall he answer them, saying, I say to you, Inasmuch as you did not do this to the least of these, you did not do it to me.

And these shall go away into everlasting punishment, but the righteous into life eternal.

The plot to kill Jesus

When Jesus had finished all these sayings, he said to his disciples,

You know that after two days is the feast of the passover, and the Son of man is to be betrayed and crucified.

Then the chief priests and the scribes and the elders of the people assembled together at the palace of the high priest, who was called Caiaphas,

And consulted that they might take Jesus by subtlety and kill him.

But they said, Not on the feast day, lest there be an uproar among the people.

Now when Jesus was in Bethany in the house of Simon, the leper,

Mary Magdalene came to him with an alabaster box of very expensive ointment and poured it on his head, as he was eating.

But when his disciples saw this, they became indignant, saying, To what purpose is this waste?

For this ointment might have been sold for much, and given to the poor.

When Jesus heard this, he said to them, Why are you troubling this woman? For she has done a good deed for me.

For the poor you have with you always, but me you do not always have.

For in that she has poured this ointment on my body, she did it for my burial.

Truly, I say to you, Wherever this gospel shall be preached in all the world, what this woman has done will be told as a memorial to her.

*   *   *

Then one of the twelve, called Judas Iscariot, went to the chief priests,

And said to them, What will you give me, if I will deliver him to you? And they agreed with him for thirty pieces of silver.

And from that time forward he sought an opportunity to betray him.

The Last Supper

On the first day of the feast of the unleavened bread, the disciples came to Jesus, saying to him, Where do you wish to eat the passover?

And he said, Go into the city, there shall a man meet you, bearing a pitcher of water; follow him into the house where he enters.

And you shall say to the owner of the house, The Master says to you, Where is the guest room, where I shall eat the passover with my disciples?

And he shall show you a large upper room furnished, there make ready.

And they went and found as he had said to them, and they made ready for the passover.

Now when the evening came, he sat down with the twelve.

And as they were eating, Jesus took bread and blessed it and broke it and gave it to the disciples and said, Take, eat; this is my body.

And he took the cup and gave thanks and gave it to them, saying, Drink all of it;

For this is my blood of the new testament, which is shed for many for the remission of sins.

But I say to you, I will not drink in the future of this fruit of the vine, until that day when I drink it new with you in my Father's kingdom.

And when supper ended, the devil went into the heart of Judas Iscariot, Simon's son, to betray him;

Jesus, knowing that the Father had given all things into his hands and that he had come from God and went to God;

He rose from supper and laid aside his garments and took a towel and girded himself.

After that he poured water into a basin and began to wash the disciples' feet and to wipe them with the towel with which he was girded.

Then he came to Simon Peter; and Peter said to him, Lord, do you wash my feet?

Jesus answered and said to him, What I do you know not now, but you shall know afterwards.

Peter said to him, You shall never wash my feet. Jesus answered him, If I do not wash you, you have no part with me.

Simon Peter said to him, Lord, not only my feet, but my hands and my head also.

Jesus said to him, He that is washed needs not except to wash his feet, but is entirely clean; and you are clean, but not all of you.

For he knew who would betray him; therefore, he said, You are not all clean.

So after he had washed their feet and had put on his

garments and was seated again, he said to them, Do you know what I have done to you?

You call me Master and Lord; and you say well, for so I am.

If I, then, your Lord and Master, have washed your feet, you ought to also wash one another's feet.

For I have given you an example, that you should do as I have done for you.

I say to you, The servant is not greater than his lord; neither he that is sent greater than he that sent him.

If you know these things, happy are you if you do them.

I speak not of all of you (I know whom I have chosen), but that the scripture may be fulfilled, He that eats bread with me has lifted up his heel against me.

Now I tell you before it happens, that, when it happens, you may believe that I am he.

I say to you, He that receives whoever I send receives me; and he that receives me receives him that sent me.

When Jesus had said this, he was troubled and said, I say to you that one of you shall betray me.

Then the disciples looked at one another, doubting what he had said.

Now there was leaning on Jesus' chest one of his disciples, whom Jesus loved.

Simon Peter, therefore, called to him, to ask him who he was referring to.

He, then, lying on Jesus' chest, said to him, Lord, who is it?

Jesus answered, He to whom I shall give a morsel when I have dipped it. And when he had dipped the morsel, he gave it to Judas Iscariot, the son of Simon.

And after the morsel Satan entered him. Then Jesus said to him, What you do, do it quickly.

Now no one at the table knew why he had said this to him.

For some of them thought, because Judas had the sack, that Jesus had said to him, Buy those things that we need for the feast; or, that he should give something to the poor.

He, then, having received the morsel, went immediately out; and it was night.

Then, when he had left, Jesus said, Now is the Son of man glorified, and God is glorified in him.

If God is glorified in him, God shall also glorify him in himself and shall straightaway glorify him.

Little children, only a little while am I with you. You shall seek me, and as I said to the Jews, Where I go, you cannot come; so now I say this to you.

A new commandment I give to you, that you love one another as I have loved you.

By this shall all men know that you are my disciples, if you have love for one another.

The following passage is Cayce's description of the Last Supper:

The Lord's Supper—here with the Master—see what they had for supper—boiled fish, rice, with leeks, wine, and loaf. One of the pitchers in which it was served was broken—the handle was broken, as was the lip to same.

The whole robe of the Master was not white, but pearl gray—all combined into one—the gift of Nicodemus to the Lord.

The better looking of the twelve, of course, was Judas, while the younger was John—oval face, dark hair, smooth face—only one with the short hair. Peter, the rough and ready—always that of very short beard, rough, and not altogether clean; while Andrew's is just the opposite—very sparse, but inclined to be long more on the side and under the chin—long on the up-

per lip—his robe was always near gray or black, while his clouts or breeches were striped; while those of Philip and Bartholomew were red and brown.

The Master's hair is 'most red, inclined to be curly in portions, yet not feminine or weak—*strong*, with heavy piercing eyes that are blue or steel-gray.

His weight would be at least a hundred and seventy pounds. Long tapering fingers, nails well kept. Long nail, though, on the left little finger.

Merry—even in the hour of trial. Joke—even in the moment of betrayal.

The sack is empty. Judas departs.

The last is given of the wine and loaf, with which He gives the emblems that should be so dear to every follower of Him. Lays aside His robe, which is all of one piece—girds the towel about His waist, which is dressed with linen that is blue and white. Rolls back the folds, kneels first before John, James, then to Peter—who refuses.

Then the dissertation as to "He that would be the greatest would be servant of all."

The basin is taken as without handle, and is made of wood. The water is from the gherkins [gourds], that are in the wide-mouth Shibboleths [streams? Judges 12:6] that stand in the house of John's father, Zebedee.

And now comes "It is finished."

They sing the ninety-first Psalm—"He that dwelleth in the secret place of the Most High shall abide under the shadow of the Almighty. I will say of the Lord, He is my refuge and my fortress: my God; in Him will I trust."

He is the musician as well, for He uses the harp.   5749-1

The following passage is the Bible's description of the events after the Last Supper:

> And when they had sung a hymn, they went out to the mount of Olives.
>
> Then Jesus said to them, All you shall be offended because of me this night; for it is written, I will strike the shepherd, and the sheep of the flock shall be scattered abroad.
>
> But after I have risen again, I will go before you into Galilee.
>
> Peter answered and said to him, Though all men shall be offended because of you, I will never be offended.
>
> Jesus said to him, I say to you that this night, before the cock crows, you shall deny me three times.
>
> Peter said to him, Though I should die with you, I will not deny you. Likewise said all the disciples.
>
> And Jesus said to the disciples, Let not your heart be troubled, you believe in God, believe also in me.
>
> In my Father's house are many mansions; if it were not so, I would have told you. I go to prepare a place for you.
>
> And if I go and prepare a place for you, I will come again and receive you to myself, that where I am, there you may be also.
>
> And where I go you know and the way you know.
>
> Thomas said to him, Lord, we do not know where you go, and how can we know the way?
>
> Jesus said to him, I am the way, the truth, and the life; no man comes to the Father, but by me.
>
> If you had known me, you should have known my Father also; and from now on you know him and have seen him.
>
> Philip said to him, Lord, show us the Father, and it will suffice us.

Jesus said to him, Have I been such a long time with you, and yet you have not known me, Philip? He that has seen me has seen the Father; then how can you say, Show us the Father?

Do you not believe that I am in the Father and the Father in me? The words that I speak to you, I speak not of myself; but the Father that lives in me, he does the works.

Believe me that I am in the Father and the Father in me; or else believe me for the very works' sake.

Truly, truly, I say to you, He that believes in me, the works that I do shall he do also; and greater works than these shall he do, because I go to my Father.

And whatever you ask in my name, that will I do, that the Father may be glorified in the Son.

If you ask anything in my name, I will do it.

If you love me, keep my commandments.

And I will pray the Father, and he shall give you another Comforter, that he may abide with you forever;

The Spirit of truth, whom the world cannot receive, because it sees him not, neither knows him, but you know him, for he lives with you and shall be in you.

I will not leave you comfortless, I will come to you.

Yet a little while, and the world sees me no more; but you see me. Because I live, you shall live also.

At that day you shall know that I am in my Father and you in me and I in you.

He that has my commandments and keeps them, he it is that loves me; and he that loves me shall be loved by my Father, and I will love him and will manifest myself to him.

Judas said to him, not Iscariot, Lord, how is it that you will manifest yourself to us and not to the world?

Jesus answered and said to him, If a man loves me, he will keep my words, and my Father will love him,

FREE CATALOG OF BOOKS
AND MEMBERSHIP ACTIVITIES

Fill-in and mail this postage-paid card today.

Please write clearly

Name: _____

Address: _____

City: _____

State/Province: _____

Postal/Zip Code: _____ Country: _____

Association for Research and Enlightenment, Inc.
215 67th Street
Virginia Beach, VA 23451-2061

For Faster Service call 1-800-723-1112
www.are-cayce.com

and we will come to him and live with him.

He that does not love me, does not keep my sayings; and the word which you hear is not mine, but the Father's, who sent me.

These things have I spoken to you, being present with you.

But the Comforter, the Holy Spirit, whom the Father will send in my name, he shall teach you all things and bring all things to your remembrance, whatever I have said to you.

Peace I leave with you, my peace I give to you; not as the world gives, I give to you. Let not your heart be troubled, neither let it be afraid.

You have heard how I said to you, I go away and come again to you. If you loved me, you would rejoice, because I said, I go to the Father; for my Father is greater than I.

And now I have told you before it comes to pass, that, when it does come to pass, you might believe.

Hereafter I will not talk much with you, for the prince of this world comes and has nothing in me.

But that the world may know that I love the Father, and, as the Father gave me commandment, even so I do. Arise, let us go from here.

* * *

I am the true vine, and my Father is the vinedresser.

Every branch in me that does not bear fruit he takes away, and every branch that bears fruit, he prunes it, so it may bring forth more fruit.

Now you are clean through the word which I have spoken to you.

Live in me and I in you. As the branch cannot bear fruit of itself, except it live on the vine, no more can you, except you live in me.

I am the vine, you are the branches. He that lives in me and I in him, the same brings forth much fruit; for without me you can do nothing.

If a man does not live in me, he is cast forth as a branch and is withered; and men gather them and throw them into the fire, and they are burned.

If you live in me and my words live in you, you shall ask what you will, and it shall be done to you.

In this is my Father glorified, that you bear much fruit; so shall you be my disciples.

As the Father has loved me, so have I loved you; continue in my love.

If you keep my commandments, you shall live in my love, even as I have kept my Father's commandments and live in his love.

These things have I spoken to you, that my joy might remain in you and that your joy might be full.

This is my commandment, that you love one another, as I have loved you.

Greater love has no man than this, than to lay down his life for his friends.

You are my friends, if you do whatever I command you.

From now on I do not call you servants; for the servant does not know what his lord does; but I have called you friends; for all things that I have heard of my Father I have made known to you.

You have not chosen me, but I have chosen you and ordained you, that you should go and bring forth fruit and that your fruit should remain; that whatever you shall ask of the Father in my name, he may give it to you.

These things I command you, that you love one another.

If the world hates you, you know that it hated me before it hated you.

If you were of the world, the world would love its own; but because you are not of the world, but I have chosen you out of the world, therefore the world hates you.

Remember the word that I said to you, The servant is not greater than his lord. If they have persecuted me, they will also persecute you; if they have kept my saying, they will keep yours also.

But all these things will they do to you for my name's sake, because they do not know him that sent me.

If I had not come and spoken to them, they would not have sin; but now they have no cloak for their sin.

He that hates me hates my Father also.

If I had not done among them the works which no other man has done, they would not have sin; but now have they both seen and hated both me and my Father.

But this happened, that the word might be fulfilled that is written in their law, They hated me without a cause.

But when the Comforter comes, whom I will send to you from the Father, the Spirit of truth, who proceeds from the Father, shall testify of me.

And you shall also bear witness, because you have been with me from the beginning.

These things I have spoken to you, that you should not be offended.

They shall put you out of the synagogues; yes, the time comes, that anyone that kills you will think that he does God a service.

And these things they will do to you, because they have not known the Father nor me.

But these things have I told you, that when the time shall come, you may remember that I told you about them. And these things I did not tell you at the beginning, because I was with you.

But now I go my way to him that sent me, and none of you asks me, Where do you go?

But because I have said these things to you, sorrow has filled your heart.

Nevertheless, I tell you the truth: It is expedient for

you that I go away; for if I do not go away, the
Comforter will not come to you; but if I depart, I will
send him to you.

And when he comes, he will convict the world of sin
and of righteousness and of judgment:

Of sin, because they did not believe in me;

Of righteousness, because I go to my Father, and
you will see me no more;

Of judgment, because the prince of this world is
judged.

I have yet many things to say to you, but you cannot
bear them now.

Nevertheless, when he, the Spirit of truth, comes,
he will guide you into all truth; for he shall not speak
of himself, but whatever he shall hear, that shall he
speak, and he will show you things to come.

He shall glorify me; for he shall receive of mine and
shall show it to you.

All things that the Father has are mine; therefore I
said, that he shall take of mine and shall show it to you.

A little while and you shall not see me; and again,
a little while and you shall see me, because I go to the
Father.

Then some of his disciples said among themselves,
What is this that he says to us, A little while and you
shall not see me; and again, a little while and you shall
see me, and, Because I go to the Father?

They said, therefore, What is this that he says, A
little while? We do not know what he means.

Now Jesus knew that they wanted to ask him and
said to them, Do you wonder what I meant when I
said, A little while and you shall not see me; and again,
a little while and you shall see me?

I say to you, You shall weep and lament, but the
world shall rejoice; and you shall be sorrowful, but
your sorrow shall be turned into joy.

A woman, when she is in labor, has sorrow, because

her hour has come; but as soon as she delivers the child, she remembers no more the anguish, for joy that a baby is born into the world.

And you now, therefore, have sorrow; but I will see you again, and your heart shall rejoice, and your joy no man will take from you.

And in that day you shall ask me nothing. I say to you, Whatever you shall ask the Father in my name, he will give you.

Before you have asked nothing in my name; ask and you shall receive, that your joy may be full.

These things have I spoken to you in proverbs; but the time comes when I shall speak no more to you in proverbs, but I shall show you plainly of the Father.

At that day you shall ask in my name and I say not to you, that I will pray the Father for you;

For the Father himself loves you, because you have loved me and have believed that I came out from God.

I came forth from the Father and am come into the world; again, I leave the world and go to the Father.

His disciples said to him, Now speak plainly and speak no proverb.

Now we are sure that you know all things, and do not need any man to ask you; by this we believe that you came forth from God.

Jesus answered them, Do you now believe?

Behold, the hour comes, yes, is now come, that you shall be scattered, every man to his own, and shall leave me alone; and yet I am not alone, because the Father is with me.

These things I have spoken to you, that in me you might have peace. In the world you shall have tribulation, but be of good cheer; I have overcome the world.

These words Jesus spoke and lifted up his eyes to heaven and said, Father, the hour has come; glorify your Son, that your Son may also glorify you.

As you have given him power over all flesh, that he should give eternal life to as many as you have given him.

And this is life eternal, that they might know you, the true God, and Jesus Christ, whom you have sent.

I have glorified you on the earth; I have finished the work which you gave me to do.

And now, O Father, glorify me with your own self with the glory which I had with you before the world was.

I have manifested your name to the men whom you gave me out of the world; yours they were, and you gave them to me, and they have kept your word.

Now they have known that all things, whatever you have given me are of you.

For I have given to them the words which you gave me; and they have received them, and have known surely that I came out from you, and they have believed that you did send me.

I pray for them; I pray not for the world, but for them whom you have given me; for they are yours.

And all mine are yours, and yours are mine; and I am glorified in them.

And now I am no more in the world, but these are in the world, and I come to you. Holy Father, keep through your own name those whom you have given me, that they may be one, as we are one.

While I was with them in the world, I kept them in your name; those that you gave me I have kept, and none of them is lost, but the son of perdition, that the scripture might be fulfilled.

And now come I to you; and these things I speak in the world, that they might have my joy fulfilled in themselves.

I have given them your word; and the world has hated them, because they are not of the world, even as I am not of the world.

I pray not that you should take them out of the world, but that you should keep them from the evil one.

They are not of the world, even as I am not of the world.

Sanctify them through your truth, your word is truth.

As you have sent me into the world, even so have I also sent them into the world.

And for their sakes I sanctify myself, that they also might be sanctified through the truth.

Neither pray I for these alone, but for them also who shall believe in me through their word;

That they all may be one, as you, Father, are in me and I in you, that they also may be one in us; that the world may believe that you have sent me.

And the glory which you gave me I have given them, that they may be one, even as we are one:

I in them and you in me, that they may be made perfect in one; and that the world may know that you have sent me and have loved them, as you have loved me.

Father, I will that they also, whom you have given me, be with me where I am, that they may behold my glory, which you have given me; for you loved me before the foundation of the world.

O righteous Father, the world has not known you; but I have known you, and these have known that you have sent me.

And I have declared to them your name and will declare it, that the love with which you have loved me may be in them and I in them.

Jesus' agony in the garden at Gethsemane

Then Jesus came with them to a place called Gethsemane and said to the disciples, Sit here, while I go and pray.

And he took Peter and the two sons of Zebedee with him and began to be sorrowful and very depressed.

Then he said to them, My soul is exceedingly sorrowful, even to death; stay here and watch with me.

And he went a little farther and fell on his face and prayed, saying, O my Father, if it be possible, let this cup pass from me; nevertheless, not as I will, but as you will.

And he came to the disciples and found them asleep; and he said to Peter, What, you could not watch with me for one hour?

Watch and pray, that you enter not into temptation; indeed the spirit is willing, but the flesh is weak.

He went away again the second time and prayed, saying, O my Father, if this cup may not pass away from me except I drink it, thy will be done.

And he came and found them asleep again; for their eyes were heavy.

And he left them and went away again and prayed the third time, saying the same words.

Then he came to his disciples and said to them, Sleep on now and take your rest; behold, the hour is at hand, and the Son of man is betrayed into the hands of sinners.

Rise, let us be going; behold, my betrayer is here.

And while he spoke, Judas came and with him a great multitude with torches and swords and clubs, from the chief priests and elders of the people.

Now he that betrayed him gave them a sign, saying, Whoever I kiss, that is he; hold him fast.

And he came to Jesus and said, Hail, master, and kissed him.

And Jesus said to him, Friend, why have you come? Then they came and laid hands on Jesus and took him.

And Peter stretched out his hand and drew his sword and struck a servant of the high priest's and cut off his ear.

Then Jesus said to him, Put up your sword, for all they that take up the sword shall perish by the sword.

Do you think that I cannot now pray to my Father, and he shall presently give me more than twelve legions of angels?

But how, then, shall the scriptures be fulfilled, that must be?

In that same hour Jesus said to the multitudes, Have you come out as against a thief with swords and clubs to take me? I sat daily with you teaching in the temple, and you laid no hold on me.

But all this was done that the scriptures of the prophets might be fulfilled. Then all the disciples forsook him and fled.

Jesus is brought before Caiaphas

And they led Jesus away to Caiaphas, the high priest, where the scribes and elders were assembled.

But Peter followed him from a distance to the high priest's court and went in and sat with the guards, to see the end.

Now the chief priests and elders and all the council sought false witness against Jesus, to put him to death,

But found none, yes, though many false witnesses came, yet they found none. At the last came two false witnesses,

And said, This man said, I am able to destroy the temple of God and to build it in three days.

And the high priest arose and said to him, Do you have an answer? What about the testimony of these witnesses?

But Jesus said nothing. And the high priest answered and said to him, I command you by the living God to tell us whether you are the Christ, the Son of God.

Jesus said to him, You have said; nevertheless, I say

to you, Hereafter you shall see the Son of man sitting on the right hand of power and coming in the clouds of heaven.

Then the high priest tore his clothes, saying, He has spoken blasphemy! What further need have we of witnesses? Now you have heard his blasphemy.

What do you think? They answered and said, He is guilty of death.

Then they spit in his face and pushed him; and others struck him with the palms of their hands, saying, Prophesy to us, you Christ, who struck you?

Now Peter sat outside in the court, and a maid came to him, saying, You also were with Jesus of Galilee.

But he denied it before them all, saying, I do not know what you mean.

And when he had gone out into the porch, another maid saw him and said to those that were there, This fellow was also with Jesus of Nazareth.

And again he denied with an oath, I do not know the man.

And after a while those that stood by came to him and said, Surely you are also one of them, for your speech betrays you.

Then he began to curse and to swear, saying, I do not know the man. And immediately the cock crowed.

And Peter remembered the words of Jesus, who said to him, Before the cock crows, you shall deny me three times. And he went out and wept bitterly.

* * *

When the morning came, all the chief priests and elders of the people took counsel against Jesus to put him to death.

And when they had bound him, they led him away and delivered him to Pontius Pilate, the Roman governor.

Then Judas, who had betrayed him, when he saw that he was condemned, repented, and brought the thirty pieces of silver to the chief priests and elders, saying, I have sinned in that I have betrayed innocent blood. And they said, What is that to us? See to it yourself.

And he threw down the pieces of silver in the temple and departed and went and hung himself.

And the chief priests took the silver pieces and said, It is not lawful to put them into the treasury, because it is the price of blood.

And they took counsel and bought with them the potter's field, to bury strangers in.

Therefore, that field was called, The field of blood to this day.

Then was fulfilled that which was spoken by Jeremiah, the prophet, saying, And they took the thirty pieces of silver, the price of him on whom a price had been set by some of the sons of Israel, and they gave them for the potter's field, as the Lord directed me.

Jesus before Pontius Pilate

And the whole multitude led Jesus to Pilate, and they began to accuse him, saying, We found this man perverting the nation and forbidding to give tribute to Caesar, saying that he himself was Christ, the king.

And Pilate asked him, saying, Are you the King of the Jews? And he answered and said, You have said it.

Then Pilate said to the chief priests and to the people, I find no fault in this man.

And they were even more fierce, saying, He stirs up the people, teaching throughout all Judea, beginning from Galilee to this place.

When Pilate heard, Galilee, he asked whether he was a Galilean.

And as soon as he realized that he belonged in Herod's jurisdiction, he sent him to Herod, who was also in Jerusalem at that time.

And when Herod saw Jesus, he was very glad, for he wanted to see him for a long time, because he had heard many things about him, and he hoped to see him do some miracle.

Then he questioned him at length, but Jesus said nothing.

And the chief priests and scribes stood by and vehemently accused him.

And Herod, with his men of war, treated him with contempt and mocked him and arrayed him in a gorgeous robe and sent him again to Pilate.

And that same day Pilate and Herod became friends, where before they had been enemies.

And Pilate, when he had called together the chief priests and the rulers and the people, said to them, You have brought this man to me as one that perverts the people, and I, having examined him before you, have found no fault in him concerning those things which you accuse him of.

No, nor Herod either, for I sent you to him, and nothing worthy of death has been done by him.

I will, therefore, chastise him and release him.

(For of necessity he must release one prisoner to them at the feast.)

And they all cried out at once, saying, Away with this man and release to us Barabbas (who was thrown into prison for sedition and murder).

Pilate, therefore, was willing to release Jesus and spoke to them again.

But they cried, Crucify him! Crucify him!

And he said to them a third time, Why, what evil has he done? I find no reason to put him to death. I will, therefore, chastise him and let him go.

And they were urgent with loud voices, saying that he must be crucified. And their voices prevailed.

When Pilate saw that he could gain nothing and that a riot was at hand, he took water and washed his hands before the multitude, saying, I am innocent of the blood of this just man. See to it yourselves.

Then all the people answered him and said, His blood be on us and on our children.

Then he released Barabbas to them, and when he had scourged Jesus, he delivered him to be crucified.

Jesus is crucified

Then the soldiers of the governor took Jesus into the common hall and gathered a whole band of soldiers.

And they stripped him and put a scarlet robe on him.

And when they had made a crown of thorns, they put it on his head and a reed in his right hand, and they bowed their knees before him and mocked him, saying, Hail, King of the Jews!

And they spit on him and took the reed and struck him on the head.

And after they had mocked him, they took the robe off him and put his own clothes on him and led him away to be crucified.

And as they led him away, they grabbed one Simon of Cyrene, and on him they laid the cross, that he might bear it after Jesus.

And a great company of people followed him, women, who wailed and lamented him.

And there were also two others, criminals, led with him to be put to death.

And they went forth to a place called Golgotha, which means, the place of the skull,

Where they crucified him and the two others with him, one on one side and one on the other, with Jesus in the center.

And Jesus said, Father, forgive them, for they know not what they do.

And Pilate wrote a title and put it on the cross. And it said, JESUS OF NAZARETH, THE KING OF THE JEWS.

The title was read by many of the Jews, for the place where Jesus was crucified was near the city, and it was written in Hebrew, Greek, and Latin.

Then the chief priests of the Jews said to Pilate, Do not write, The King of the Jews, but that he said, I am King of the Jews.

But Pilate answered, What I have written, I have written.

And one of the criminals, who were hanged, railed at him, saying, If you are the Christ, save yourself and us.

But the other, answering, rebuked him, saying, Do you not fear God, since you are under the same death sentence?

For we, indeed, have received the due reward for our deeds. But this man has done nothing wrong.

And he said to Jesus, Lord, remember me when you come into your kingdom.

And Jesus said to him, Truly, I say to you, today you shall be with me in paradise.

Then the soldiers, when they had crucified Jesus, took his garments and made four parts, to every soldier a part; and also his robe. Now the robe was without seam, woven from the top to bottom.

They said among themselves, Let us not tear it, but cast lots for it, for whose it shall be; that the scripture might be fulfilled which said, They parted my garments among them, and for my clothing they did cast lots. And the soldiers did this.

Now standing by the cross of Jesus was his mother and his mother's sister, Mary, the wife of Cleophas, and Mary Magdalene.

When Jesus saw his mother and the disciple standing by, whom he loved, he said to his mother, Woman, behold your son!

Then he said to the disciple, Behold your mother! And from that hour forward the disciple took her into his own home.

Now from the sixth hour there was darkness over all the land until the ninth hour. And about the ninth hour Jesus cried with a loud voice, My God, my God, why hast thou forsaken me?

After this Jesus, knowing that all was now accomplished, that the scripture might be fulfilled, said, I thirst.

A bowl full of vinegar stood by, so they put a sponge full of vinegar on a stick and held it to his mouth.

When Jesus received the vinegar, he said, It is finished. And he bowed his head and gave up the spirit.

And, behold, the veil of the temple was torn in two from the top to the bottom, and the earth did quake, and rocks were split.

And the graves were opened, and many bodies of the saints that slept were raised,

And came out of the graves after his resurrection, and went into the holy city, and appeared to many.

Now when the centurion and those that were with him watching Jesus saw the earthquake and those things that happened, they were afraid and said, Truly, this man was the Son of God.

* * *

Because it was the preparation, the Jews asked Pilate if their legs could be broken (so that the bodies would not remain on the cross on the sabbath day, that was a high day).

Then the soldiers came and broke the legs of the first and of the other who was crucified with him.

But when they came to Jesus and saw that he was dead already, they did not break his legs.

But one of the soldiers with a spear pierced his side, and immediately there came out blood and water.

For these things were done, that the scripture might be fulfilled, A bone of him shall not be broken.

And, again, another scripture says, They shall look on him whom they pierced.

Jesus is buried

At evening time, there came a rich man of Arimathea, named Joseph, who was also a disciple of Jesus;

He went to Pilate and begged for the body of Jesus. Then Pilate commanded the body to be delivered.

And when Joseph had taken the body, he wrapped it in a clean linen cloth, and Nicodemus came also, bringing a mixture of myrrh and aloes, about a hundred pounds weight. They took the body of Jesus and bound it in linen cloths with the spices as is the burial custom of the Jews,

And laid it in Joseph's new tomb, which he had hewn out of rock, and they rolled a great stone to the door of the tomb and departed.

And there were Mary Magdalene and the other Mary sitting over against the tomb.

Now the day after the day of the preparation, the chief priests and Pharisees came to Pilate,

Saying, Sir, we remember that that deceiver said, while he was alive, After three days I will rise again.

Command, therefore, that the tomb be made secure until the third day, lest his disciples come by night and steal him away and say to the people, He is risen from the dead; so that the last error shall be worse than the first.

Pilate said to them, You have a guard, go your way, make it as secure as you can.

So they went and made the tomb secure, sealing the stone and placing guard.

Jesus' resurrection

At the end of the sabbath, as it began to dawn on the first day of the week, Mary Magdalene and the other Mary came to see the tomb.

And, behold, there was a great earthquake, for an angel of the Lord descended from heaven and came and rolled back the stone from the door and sat upon it.

His countenance was like lightning and his raiment white as snow;

And for fear of him the guards shook and became as dead men.

And the angel answered and said to the women, Fear not, for I know that you seek Jesus, who was crucified.

He is not here, for he is risen, as he said. Come, see the place where the Lord lay.

And go quickly, and tell his disciples that he is risen from the dead; and behold, he goes before you into Galilee. There shall you see him.

And they left quickly from the tomb with fear and great joy and ran to tell his disciples.

But Mary Magdalene stood outside the tomb weeping, and as she wept, she stooped down and looked into the tomb.

And saw two angels in white sitting, one at the head and the other at the feet, where the body of Jesus had lain.

And they said to her, Woman, why are you crying? She said to them, Because they have taken away my Lord, and I do not know where they have laid him.

And when she had said this, she turned back and saw Jesus standing and did not know that it was Jesus.

Jesus said to her, Woman, why are you crying? Whom do you seek? She, supposing him to be the gardener, said to him, Sir, if you have taken him from here, tell me where you have laid him, and I will take him away.

Jesus said to her, Mary. She turned and said to him, Master.

Jesus said to her, Touch me not, for I have not yet ascended to my Father. But go to my brothers and say to them, I ascend to my Father and your Father and to my God and your God.

Mary Magdalene went and told the disciples that she had seen Jesus and that he had spoken these things to her.

Cayce tells us that if Mary had touched Jesus at that time, it would have been like grabbing a high-voltage electric wire.

The walk to Emmaus

And two of the disciples went that same day to a village called Emmaus, which was about seven miles from Jerusalem.

And they talked together of all the things that had happened.

And while they communed together and reasoned, Jesus himself drew near and went with them. But they did not recognize him.

And he said to them, What are you talking about, as you walk with one another and are sad?

And one of them, whose name was Cleopas, answered and said to him, Are you a stranger in Jerusalem and do not know what has happened there in the past few days?

And he said to them, What things? And they said to him, Concerning Jesus of Nazareth, who was a prophet, mighty in deed and word before God and all the people;

And how the chief priests and our rulers delivered him to be condemned to death and have crucified him.

But we hoped that it would be he who redeemed Israel; and, besides all this, today is the third day since these things happened.

Yes, and certain women of our company amazed us, for earlier they were at the tomb, and when they could not find his body, they came, saying that they had seen a vision of angels, who said that he was alive.

And some of those who were with us went to the tomb and found it empty as the women had said.

Then he said to them, O foolish men and slow of heart to believe all that the prophets have spoken!

Ought not Christ to have suffered these things and to enter into his glory?

And beginning with Moses and all the prophets, he explained to them, in all the scriptures, the things concerning himself.

And they drew near to the village where they were going, and he indicated that he would go farther on.

But they constrained him, saying, Stay with us; for it is almost evening, and the day is over. And he went in to stay with them.

And as he sat eating with them, he took bread and blessed it and broke it and gave it to them.

And their eyes were opened, and they recognized him, and he vanished out of their sight.

And they said to each other, Did not our hearts burn within us, while he talked with us along the way and while he opened to us the scriptures?

* * *

On the evening of that same day, where the disciples assembled and the doors were shut for fear of the Jews, Jesus came and stood with them and said to them, Peace be to you.

And when he had said this, he showed them his hands and his side. Then the disciples were glad, when they saw the Lord.

Then Jesus said to them again, Peace be to you, as my Father has sent me, I send you.

And when he had said this, he breathed on them and said to them, Receive the Holy Spirit;

Whoever's sins you remit, they are remitted to them, and whoever's sins you retain, they are retained.

And while they were still in a state of disbelief and wondering, he said to them, Have you anything to eat?

And they gave him a piece of broiled fish and a honeycomb.

And he took it and ate it before them.

Doubting Thomas

But Thomas, one of the twelve, called Didymus, was not with them when Jesus came.

The other disciples, therefore, said to him, We have seen the Lord. But Thomas said to them, Except I shall see in his hands the print of the nails and put my finger into the print of the nails and thrust my hand into his side, I will not believe.

And after eight days, again his disciples were inside and Thomas with them; then Jesus came, the doors being shut, and stood with them and said, Peace be with you.

Then he said to Thomas, Reach here your finger, and see my hands, and reach here your hand, and thrust it into my side, and be not faithless, but believing.

And Thomas answered and said to him, My Lord and my God.

Jesus said to him, Thomas, because you have seen me, you believe; blessed are they that have not seen and yet believe.

After these things Jesus appeared again to the disciples at the Sea of Tiberias and revealed himself in this manner:

There were together Simon Peter and Thomas, called Didymus, and Nathanael, of Cana in Galilee; and the sons of Zebedee and two other disciples.

Simon Peter said to them, I am going fishing. They said to him, We will go with you. So they went out and entered into a boat immediately, but by night they had caught nothing.

And when the morning came, Jesus stood on the shore, but the disciples did not know that it was Jesus.

Then Jesus said to them, Children, do you have any food? They answered, No.

And he said to them, Cast the net on the right side of the boat, and you shall find. They cast, therefore, and now they were not able to draw it for the multitude of fish.

Then John, the disciple whom Jesus loved, said to Peter, It is the Lord. When Simon Peter heard this, he put on his coat, for he was naked, and jumped into the sea.

And the other disciples came in a boat, for they were not far from land, dragging the net with fish.

As soon as they came to land, they saw a fire of coals there and fish laid on it and bread.

Jesus said to them, Bring the fish which you have caught.

Simon Peter went up and drew the net to land full

of great fish, a hundred and fifty-three, and there were so many, yet the net was not broken.

Jesus said to them, Come dine. And none of the disciples dared ask him, Who are you? knowing that it was the Lord.

Jesus then came and took bread and gave it to them and fish likewise.

This was the third time that Jesus showed himself to his disciples, after he had risen from the dead.

So when they had eaten, Jesus said to Simon Peter, Simon, son of Jonah, do you love me more than these? Peter said, Yes, Lord, you know that I love you. He said to him, Feed my lambs.

He said to him again a second time, Simon, son of Jonah, do you love me? Peter said again, Yes, Lord, you know that I love you. He said to him, Feed my sheep.

He said to him a third time, Simon, son of Jonah, do you love me? Peter was grieved because Jesus said to him a third time, Do you love me? And Peter said to him, Lord, you know all things, you know that I love you. Jesus said to him, Feed my sheep.

I say to you, When you were young, you girded yourself and walked where you would, but when you grow old, you shall stretch forth your hands and another shall gird you and carry you where you do not want to go.

He said this to signify by what death he should glorify God. And when he had said this, he said to Peter, Follow me.

Then Peter, turning about, saw John, the disciple whom Jesus loved, following and said, Lord, who is he that betrays you?

Peter, seeing him, said to Jesus, Lord, and what shall this man do?

Jesus said to him, If I will that he stay till I come, what is that to you? Follow me.

Then this saying went abroad among the disciples

that John should not die. Yet Jesus did not say to him, He shall not die, but, If I will that he stay till I come, what is that to you?

Cayce's view on the Resurrection

Cayce explains the nature and meaning of the Resurrection in the following readings:

Q. Is the transmutation of human flesh to flesh divine the real mystery of the Crucifixion and Resurrection? Explain this mystery.
A. **There is no mystery to the transmutation of the body of the Christ. For having attained in the physical consciousness the at-onement with the Father-Mother-God, the completeness was such that with the disintegration of the body—as indicated in the manner in which the shroud, the robe, the napkin lay—there was then the taking of the body-physical form. This was the manner. It was not a transmutation, as of changing from one to another.**

Just as indicated in the manner in which the body-physical entered the Upper Room with the doors closed, not by being a part of the wood through which the body passed but by forming from the ether waves that were within the room, because of a meeting prepared by faith. For as had been given, "Tarry ye in Jerusalem—in the upper chamber—until *ye* be endued with power from on high."

As indicated in the spoken word to Mary in the garden, "Touch me not, for I have not yet ascended to my Father." The body (flesh) that formed that seen by the normal or carnal eye of Mary was such that it could not be handled until there had been the conscious union with the

sources of all power, of all force.

But afterward—when there had been the first, second, third, fourth and even the sixth meeting—He *then* said: "Put forth thy hand and touch the nail prints in my hands, in my feet. Thrust thy hand into my side and *believe*." This indicated the transformation.

For as indicated when the soul departs from a body (this is not being spoken of the Christ, you see), it has all of the form of the body from which it has passed—yet it is not visible to the carnal mind unless that mind has been, and is, attuned to the infinite. Then it appears, in the infinite, as that which may be handled, with all the attributes of the physical being; with the appetites, until these have been accorded to a unit of activity with universal consciousness.

Just as it was with the Christ-body: "Children, have ye anything here to eat?" This indicated to the disciples and the Apostles present that this was not transmutation but a regeneration, re-creation of the atoms and cells of body that might, through desire, masticate material things—fish and honey (in the honeycomb) were given.

As also indicated later, when He stood by the sea and the disciples and Apostles who saw Him from the distance could not, in the early morning light, discern—but when He spoke, the voice made the impression upon the mind of the beloved disciple such that he spoke, "It is the Lord!" The body had prepared fire upon the earth—fire, water, the elements that make for creation. For as the spirit is the beginning, water combined of elements is the mother of creation.

Not transmutation of flesh but creation, in the pattern indicated.

Just as when there are those various realms

about the solar system in which each entity may
find itself when absent from the body, it takes on
in those other realms not an earthly form but a
pattern—conforming to the same dimensional
elements of that individual planet or space.

2533-8

The following Cayce reading gives even more insight
into the Resurrection:

Mrs. Cayce: As we approach this Easter season our
thoughts turn naturally toward the Biblical accounts
of the resurrection of Jesus, the Christ. We seek at
this time through this channel information dealing
either with a completion of the historical account or
interpretation and explanation of the full meaning
of the resurrection which will help us to better un-
derstand and appreciate it.

Mr. Cayce: Yes. In seeking ye shall find. In the
experience of each soul that has named the name
of the Christ, this should be a season of rededi-
cation of self as being a true messenger of His in
and among men.

In seeking, then, to know more of that, as to
those here, much may be revealed to those that
in their inner selves experienced that material
period when *He*, Jesus, walked in the earth.

But for what purpose is this season observed,
that caused or called for such a sacrifice that life
might be made manifest? Is it not fitting that to
those here, to those there in that land, it came at
that particular season when life in its manifesta-
tions was being demonstrated in the material
things about each soul?

How, why, was there the need for there to be a
resurrection? Why came He into the earth to die
the death, even on the Cross? Has it been, then,

the fulfillment of promise, the fulfillment of law, the fulfillment of man's estate? Else why did He put on flesh and come into the earth in the form of man, but to be one with the Father; to show to man *his* (man's) divinity, man's relationship to the Maker; to show man that indeed the Father meant it when He said, "If ye call I will hear. Even though ye be far away, even though ye be covered with sin, if ye be washed in the blood of the lamb ye may come back."

Then, though He were the first of man, the first of the sons of God in spirit, in flesh, it became necessary that He fulfill *all* those associations, those connections that were to wipe away in the experience of man that which separates him from his Maker.

Though man be far afield, then, though he may have erred, there is established that which makes for a closer, closer walk *with* Him, through that one who experienced all those turmoils, strifes, desires, urges that may be the lot of man in the earth. Yet He put on flesh, made *Himself* as naught—even as was promised throughout, to those who walked and talked with God.

In the history, then, of the resurrection as ye have recorded in part, may it be so interpreted that those here, now, that experienced (through that period of their advent) His suffering, may—as Andrew, Martha, Naomi, Loda [?], Elois [?], Phoenix [?], Phoebe [?]—again see those days. Though there were fears from the elements without, from the political powers that made for fears of body and mind, there were the rememberings that *He* had given, "Though ye destroy this temple, in three days it will rise again."

And then as He hung upon the Cross, He called to those that He loved and remembered not only their spiritual purposes but their material lives. For He indeed in suffering the death on the Cross became the whole, the entire way; *the* way, *the* life, *the* understanding, that we who believe on Him may, too, have the everlasting life. For He committed unto those of His brethren not only the care of the spiritual life of the world but the material life of those that were of His own flesh, His own blood. Yea, as He gave His physical blood that doubt and fear might be banished, so He overcame death; not only in the physical body but in the *spirit* body—that it may become as *one* with Him, even as on that resurrection morn—that ye call thy Eastertide.

It is that breaking forth from the tomb, as exemplified in the bulb of the tree of nature itself breaking forth from the sleep that it may rise as He with healing in its very life, to bring all phases of man's experience to His Consciousness—that indeed became then the fulfilling of the law.

On what wise, then, ye ask, did this happen in materiality? Not only was He dead in body, but the soul was separated from that body. As all phases of man in the earth are made manifest, the physical body, the mental body, the soul body became as each dependent upon their own experience. Is it any wonder that the man cried, "My God, my God, *why* has thou forsaken me?"

Each soul comes to stand as He before that throne of his Maker, with the deeds that have been done in the body, in the mind, presenting the body-spiritual before that throne of mercy, before that throne of the Maker, the Creator, the God.

Yet as He, the Father, hath given to each of you, "I have given my angels charge concerning thee, and they shall bear thee up, and thou shall not know corruption."

This He demonstrated in the experience of thy Brother, thy Savior, thy Jesus, thy Christ; that would come and dwell in the hearts and lives of you all—if you will but let Him, if you will but invite Him, if you will but open thy own heart, each of you, that He may enter and abide with you.

Hence when those of His loved ones and those of His brethren came on that glad morning when the tidings had come to them, those that stood guard heard a fearful noise and saw a light, and— "the stone has been rolled away!" Then they entered into the garden, and there Mary first saw her *risen* Lord. Then came they of His brethren with the faithful women, those that loved His mother, those that were her companions in sorrow, those that were making preparations that the law might be kept that even there might be no desecration of the ground about His tomb. They, too, of His friends, His loved ones, His brethren, saw the angels.

How, why, took they on form? That there might be implanted into their hearts and souls that *fulfillment* of those promises.

What separates ye from seeing the Glory even of Him that walks with thee oft in the touch of a loving hand, in the voice of those that would comfort and cheer? For He, thy Christ, is oft with thee.

Doubt, fear, unbelief; fear that thou art not worthy!

Open thine eyes and behold the Glory, even of thy Christ present here, now, in thy midst! even as He appeared to them on that day!

What meaneth the story of the Christ, of His

resurrection, of the man Jesus that walked in Galilee, without that resurrection morn?

Little, more than that of the man thou thinkest so little of, that though his body-physical touched the bones of Elisha he walked again among men!

Dost thou believe that He has risen? How spoke Thomas? "Until I see, until I have put my hand in his side where I saw water and blood gush forth, until I have handled his body, I will *not* believe."

Ye, too, oft doubt; ye, too, oft fear. Yet He is surely with thee. And when ye at this glad season rededicate thy life, thy body, thy mind to His service, ye—too—may know, as they, that He *lives*—and is at the right hand of God to make intercession for *you*—if ye will believe; if ye will believe that He is, ye may experience. For as many as have named the name, and that do unto their brethren the deeds that bring to them (to you) that closeness, oneness of purpose with Him, may know—ye, too—in body, in mind, that He *lives today*, and will come and receive you unto Himself, that where He is there ye may be also.

Crucify Him not in thy mind nor in thy bodily activities. Be not overcome by those things that are of the earth-earthy. Rather clothe thy body, thy mind, with the thoughts, the deeds, the privileges that His suffering as a man brought to thee, that He indeed might be the first of those that slept, the first of those that came in the flesh, that passed through all those periods of preparation in the flesh, even as thou.

But if ye would put on Him, ye must claim His promises as thine own. And how canst thou claim them unless ye in thine own knowledge, thine own consciousness, *have* done—do do from day

**to day—that thy heart has told and does tell thee
is in keeping with what He has promised?**

**For thy Christ, thy Lord, thy Jesus, is nigh
unto thee—just now!**   **5749-6**

The Ascension

After appearing to and being with the disciples for
forty days, Jesus gathered five hundred of His followers
on the mount of Olives for His ascension.

So when they had come together, they asked him,
saying, Lord will you at this time restore the kingdom
to Israel?

And he said to them, It is not for you to know the
times or the seasons, which the Father has put in his
own power.

But you shall receive power, after the Holy Spirit
has come upon you, and you shall be witnesses for me
both in Jerusalem and in all Judea and in Samaria and
to the farthest reaches of the earth.

And when he had said these things, while they
watched, he was taken up, and a cloud received him
out of their sight.

And while they looked steadfastly toward heaven as
he went up, two men stood by them in white apparel;

Who said, Men of Galilee, why do you stand gazing
up into heaven? This same Jesus, who is taken up from
you into heaven, shall so come in like manner as you
have seen him go into heaven.